The Drum Theatre P

and

Birmingham Reperto

present

THROUGH A CLOUD

by Jack Shepherd

First performance on Monday 25 October 2004
at the Drum Theatre Plymouth

Thursday 21 October to Saturday 6 November 2004
at the Drum Theatre Plymouth

DRUM THEATRE PLYMOUTH

ROYAL PARADE | PLYMOUTH | PL1 2TR

Wednesday 10 November to Saturday 27 November 2004
at Birmingham Repertory Theatre, The Door

Birmingham Repertory Theatre

CAST

DAVID PEART	OLIVER CROMWELL
JACK SHEPHERD	JOHN MILTON
JODY WATSON	KATHERINE WOODSTOCK
PETER KELLY	GEORGE GREEN
DARREN LAKE	THE GUARD

JACK SHEPHERD	WRITER
SIMON STOKES	DIRECTOR
ROBIN DON	DESIGNER
JASON TAYLOR	LIGHTING DESIGNER
RICHARD PRICE	SOUND DESIGNER
SALLY COLEMAN	DEPUTY STAGE MANAGER
DARREN LAKE	ASSISTANT STAGE MANAGER

Sets, props and costumes made by TR2 – Theatre Royal Plymouth
Production Centre

DAVID PEART OLIVER CROMWELL

David trained at LAMDA and received the Rodney Millington award.

Theatre includes: GAMEPLAN (Manchester Library); THE TAMING OF THE SHREW, THE MERCHANT OF VENICE (RSC USA Tour); ARMS AND THE MAN, THE TEMPEST, WAITING FOR GODOT, THE CRUCIBLE (Mercury Theatre Colchester); ROSENCRANTZ AND GUILDERNSTERN ARE DEAD (National Tour); MEASURE FOR MEASURE (English Touring); THE INVISIBLE WOMAN (Gate Theatre); COMMUNICATING DOORS, THE LIFE OF GALILEO (Manchester Library); A GOING CONCERN (Nuffield Theatre Southampton); OUTSIDE EDGE (Derby Playhouse); LULU (Watford Palace); TWELFTH NIGHT (Lancaster Playhouse); HAMLET (Theatr Clywd); WAY UPSTREAM (Worcester Swan); THE CARETAKER (Theatre Royal Plymouth); HEDDA GABLER (Lincoln Theatre Royal); ABSURD PERSON SINGULAR (Chester Gateway); THE TAMING OF THE SHREW (Liverpool Everyman); GUYS AND DOLLS (Northcott Exeter); THE ICEMAN COMETH (Bristol Old Vic).

JACK SHEPHERD JOHN MILTON

Jack started out as an art student, studied acting at the Central School and then at the Drama Centre, which as a student he helped to found. He was a leading actor at the Royal Court Theatre in the sixties, and at the National Theatre in Bill Bryden's Cottesloe Company in the late seventies and early eighties; featuring in such productions as THE MYSTERIES, LARK RISE, AMERICAN BUFFALO, THE ICEMAN COMETH and winning an award for his performance as Roma in David Mamet's GLENGARRY GLEN ROSS.

He has appeared in many television plays over the years and in a variety of films from VIRGIN SOLDIERS in 1969 to WONDERLAND in 1999. He has also been involved in three major television series over the years BILL BRAND in 1976; BLIND JUSTICE in 1987; and more recently WYCLIFFE which filmed its last episode in 1998.

JODY WATSON   KATHERINE WOODSTOCK

Jody is a graduate of Central School of Speech and Drama.

Her theatre credits include: Regine in GHOSTS (ETT); Chase in NIGHTINGALE & CHASE (Royal Court Theatre Upstairs); Joan in THE THOUGHTS OF JOAN OF ARC ON THE ENGLISH AS SHE BURNS AT THE STAKE (RSC at the Young Vic); LOVEPLAY (RSC); Daisy and Connie in BEST MATES (RNT on tour); Dorcas in A PENNY FOR A SONG (OSC); Polly in SPARKLESHARK (RNT); and for Birmingham Repertory Theatre the title role in SAINT JOAN, Ella in CONFIDENCE, Nessie in DOWN RED LANE, and A CHRISTMAS CAROL.

Television includes: Mrs Gray in DISTANT SHORES (Yorkshire TV); Louise in MYSTERY OF MEN and DALZIEL AND PASCOE (BBC).

Prior to training, Jody was a member of the Chicken-Shed Theatre Company and Chorus with the English National Opera at the London Coliseum.

PETER KELLY   GEORGE GREEN

Peter most recently appeared in Michel Tremblay's two-hander IF ONLY at the Lyceum theatre in Edinburgh. He was in A MIDSUMMER NIGHT'S DREAM and ANTHONY AND CLEOPATRA with the RSC and his London theatre appearances include David Pownall's MASTER CLASS as Prokofiev, BROTHERS KARAMAZOV as Smerdiakov, THE GOVERNMENT INSPECTOR, CRIME AND PUNISHMENT, CORIOLANUS and the musical WHAT ABOUT LUV.

His television work includes A TOUCH OF FROST, HEARTS AND BONES, EASTENDERS, TAGGART and MINDER.

He was in the films WELCOME TO SARAJEVO, THE TALL GUY, SURVIVING PICCASSO and THE VIRGIN SOLDIERS which was the last time he worked with Jack Shepherd.

DARREN LAKE   THE GUARD / ASSISTANT STAGE MANAGER

Darren has performed mainly in musicals with main roles in shows such as WEST SIDE STORY, MAGGIE MAY, THE HIRED MAN, OH! WHAT A LOVELY WAR, ANIMAL FARM and CHESS. He has played the leads in BYE BYE BIRDIE, SWEENEY TODD, CYRANO DE BERGERAC and THE SECRET GARDEN. Television includes: GOING LIVE! and THE VET.

Films include DROWNED and THE HANGED MAN. He sang the leads on the Original Cast Recordings of KORCZAK (which toured England and Poland) and STARCHILD. He has performed with various projects in France, Belgium, Holland and Germany.
He was awarded the Individual Performance Award at the 1992 Barclays Award's held at the National Theatre. He has hosted several charity events, including many for the Theatre Royal Plymouth and was host of the Orange Festival on Plymouth Hoe, for the Queen's Golden Jubilee.
He has directed for many amateur groups, and has been director of the University of Plymouth Music Theatre Company for the last four years. He has also been working backstage at the Theatre Royal Plymouth for 5 years.

JACK SHEPHERD   WRITER

Jack began writing in the sixties; comedy sketches mainly and plays that never saw the light of day. A series of devised works followed starting with THE INCREDIBLE JOURNEY OF SIR FRANCIS YOUNG HUSBAND at the Theatre Upstairs in the late sixties and culminating with REAL TIME (Joint Stock production, 1982). A succession of stage plays including IN LAMBETH (1989) and CHASING THE MOMENT, a play about jazz musicians in 1994, both plays winning *Time Out* awards. COMIC CUTS was written for Triptych Theatre in 1996, and HALF MOON, (a play about artists in Bohemian London) was written in 1998 and performed in November of that year at the Southwark Playhouse.

He wrote several plays for television in the seventies when such a thing was possible, and a single play for radio in 1996, CRY WOLF.

SIMON STOKES DIRECTOR

Simon Stokes is Artistic Director at the Theatre Royal Plymouth.
He was Artistic Director at the Bush Theatre from the mid-70s to
the late 80s. Thereafter, alongside a freelance career, he was an Artistic
Associate and Director of Development for the Turnstyle Group in
London's West End. A new play specialist, he developed and directed
many of our now established playwrights, along with a generation of
now leading actors. He trained at the Bristol Old Vic Theatre School
and has directed in Germany, Switzerland, Israel and the USA, as well
as the UK. His most highly profiled work has included the West End
successes WHEN I WAS A GIRL I USED TO SCREAM AND SHOUT
by Sharman Macdonald (with Julie Walters, Geraldine James and Dawn
French) at the Whitehall Theatre and A SLIP OF THE TONGUE by
Dusty Hughes (with John Malkovich and Ingeborga Dapkunaite) at
the Shaftesbury Theatre. As an occasional actor he has played
Edward in Richard Eyre's film THE PLOUGHMAN'S LUNCH,
scripted by Ian McEwan, opposite Jonathan Pryce and Tim Curry, and
is beaten up by Jennifer Saunders as Saffy's lecherous lecturer Gerald
in the penultimate episode of ABSOLUTELY FABULOUS.

He most recently directed Doug Lucie's play THE GREEN MAN
which enjoyed a successful run at the Drum Theatre Plymouth prior
to transferring to the Bush Theatre, London.

ROBIN DON DESIGNER

Theatre credits include: STEPPING OUT (West Yorkshire Playhouse);
KISS OF THE SPIDERWOMAN (Bush); TICKET OF LEAVE MAN
(RNT); LES ENFANTS DU PARADIS (Royal Shakespeare Company);
A WALK IN THE WOODS (Comedy Theatre); FOOL FOR LOVE
(Donmar) and TOP GIRLS (Citizens Theatre, Glasgow).

Musicals include: ROCKY HORROR SHOW (Piccadilly); SONG AND
DANCE (Palace) ZIEGFELD (Palladium); THE BOY FRIEND (Old Vic).

Opera and Ballet includes: productions for Lyric Opera of Chicago,
Opera North, WNO, Aldeburgh Festival, San Francisco Opera, Royal
Opera House, Opera de Lyon, Sydney Opera House and Quanzhou
Ballet, China.

Film includes: THE WINTER GUEST, with Oscar-winner Emma
Thompson (directed by Alan Rickman); CARMEN.

Robin's design for the Almeida Theatre's THE WINTER GUEST
received the 1996 British Theatre Managers' Award for Best
Designer. In the same year the Critics' Circle named Robin Designer
of the Year. For Britain he won the Golden Troika at the 1992 Prague
International Theatre Design Quadrienalle.

JASON TAYLOR LIGHTING DESIGNER

Recent work includes: ABIGAIL'S PARTY (Hampstead Theatre); MY NIGHT WITH REG, DEALER'S CHOICE (Birmingham Repertory Theatre); THE CLEARING (Shared Experience); SINGLE SPIES (National Tour); SITTING PRETTY (National Tour); PIRATES OF PENZANCE (National Tour); OFFICE (Edinburgh International Festival); HEDDA GABLER, SNAKE IN FRIDGE (Royal Exchange Theatre); last year's LABOUR PARTY CONFERENCE, THE DEAD EYE BOY (Hampstead Theatre); IOLANTHE, THE MIKADO and YEOMAN OF THE GUARD (Savoy).

Jason has lit over 150 other productions including: 12 seasons at the Open Air Theatre, KINDERTRANSPORT (Vaudeville Theatre); ROSENCRANTZ AND GUILDENSTERN (Piccadilly Theatre); AND THEN THERE WHERE NONE (Duke Of York's Theatre); GREAT BALLS OF FIRE (Cambridge Theatre). Other London work includes productions at The Bush, Hampstead, the Bridewell and numerous productions for Soho Theatre.

Jason has also designed at most major regional theatres including Nottingham, Sheffield, Theatre Royal Plymouth, West Yorkshire Playhouse, Birmingham Repertory Theatre, Edinburgh, Scarborough, Southampton, Clwyd and Liverpool.

Jason was also lighting consultant for the new Soho Theatre, London and the Open Air Theatre, Regent's Park.

RICHARD PRICE SOUND DESIGNER

Richard completed several successful rock and roll tours up and down the country after University. From here he went on to the MAC in Birmingham and later onto the Belgrade Theatre in Coventry. Theatre includes: LEADER OF THE PACK, GOOD COMPANIONS, LIMESTONE COWBOY, 3 MINUTE HEROES, THE WEDDING and several pantomimes (The Belgrade); THE CRUCIBLE, EAST IS EAST, THE WIZARD OF OZ, PETER PAN, A LITTLE NIGHT MUSIC and UNSUITABLE GIRLS (Leicester Haymarket Theatre). In 2002 and 2003 Richard designed and operated the sound for MARDI GRAS and SOLID GOLD at the Ibiza Marquee.

In 2003 Richard was appointed as Head of Sound at the Theatre Royal Plymouth. Recent credits include Sound Designer on DICK WHITTINGTON and YEOMAN OF THE GUARD.

DRUM THEATRE PLYMOUTH

For the past five years the Drum Theatre Plymouth has become a driving force in the South West, pioneering new forms of stage writing, physical theatre and other innovative work. As part of the Theatre Royal Plymouth, it has taken a leading role in the national development of writing, directing and producing relationships.

Recent productions have included *Edward Gant's Amazing feats of Loneliness* by Anthony Neilson, *The Green Man* by Doug Lucie, which subsequently moved to The Bush Theatre London, *Mr Placebo* in collaboration with the Traverse Theatre Edinburgh, *Rabbit* by Brendan Cowell, a co-production with our long term associates Frantic Assembly and Gregory Burke's highly acclaimed *The Straits* in a co-production with Paines Plough and Hampstead Theatre, London.

We have recently enjoyed a successful run of Anthony Neilson's new play *The Wonderful World of Dissocia* produced with the Edinburgh International Festival, in association with The Tron Glasgow and early next year we collaborate again with Paines Plough on Philip Ridley's vigorous new play *Mercury Fur.*

The Theatre Royal itself has just produced Yukio Ninagawa's new English language *Hamlet* for national autumn touring and a spell at the Barbican Theatre London. We also recently produced and launched a new production of *Miss Saigon* for Cameron Mackintosh and national touring while our co-productions of *Jailhouse Rock* plays the Piccadilly Theatre in the West End and *Footloose The Musical* tours national prior to West End opening.

Concluding on a happy note, we are delighted that the Theatre Royal Plymouth has been voted *Best Regional Theatre 2004* in a national survey by the UK's leading theatre website *WhatsOnStage.com* involving 10,000 theatregoers and critics across the country.

Chief Executive **Adrian Vinken**
General Manager **Alan Finch**
Artistic Director **Simon Stokes**
Head of Production and Technical **Paul Clay**

www.theatreroyal.com

BIRMINGHAM REPERTORY THEATRE COMPANY

Birmingham Repertory Theatre is one of Britain's leading national theatre companies. From its base in Birmingham, The REP produces over twenty new productions each year. Under the Artistic Direction of Jonathan Church, The REP is enjoying great success with a busy and exciting programme.

Over the last few years The REP's productions have included David Hare's trilogy of plays (*Racing Demon*, *Murmuring Judges* & *The Absence of War*), Steinbeck's *Of Mice And Men*, Miller's *A View From The Bridge*, *The Wizard Of Oz*, Ibsen's *A Doll's House* and the world premieres of Alistair Beaton's *Follow My Leader* and Simon Gray's *The Old Masters*. This Autumn has seen new productions of Fernando De Rojas's *Celestina*, directed by Calixto Bieito in association with Edinburgh International Festival and Arthur Miller's *The Crucible*, which is currently on a national tour. Christmas 2004 will see a new production of Roald Dahl's *The Witches* as well as the return of The REP's original production of *The Snowman*, which has been delighting audiences in the West End for many years.

The commissioning and production of new work lies at the core of The REP's programme. In 1998 the company launched The Door, a venue exclusively dedicated to the production and presentation of new work. In 2004, The REP won the Peggy Ramsey Award, which will support the continuing development and commissioning of writers. One example of this is the world premiere a new black comedy *Behzti (Dishonour)* by Gurpreet Kaur Bhatti whose critically-acclaimed first play *Behsharam (Shameless)* played to full houses in both The Door and Soho Theatre in London. *Behzti (Dishonour)* can be seen in The Door this December.

Developing new and particularly younger audiences is also at the heart of The REP's work, in its various Education initiatives, such as Transmissions, The Young REP, Page To Stage, as well as with the programming of work in The Door for children.

Birmingham Repertory Theatre productions regularly transfer to London and tour nationally and internationally. The REP's acclaimed production of Steinbeck's *Of Mice And Men* opened in the West End in 2003. Last year's collaboration with the Edinburgh International Festival - *Hamlet*, directed by Calixto Bieito, toured to Barcelona and Dublin following performances at the festival and in Birmingham. Previous productions that have been seen in London in recent years include *The Old Masters*, *The Snowman*, *Two Pianos, Four Hands*, *Baby Doll*, *My Best Friend*, *Terracotta*, *The Gift*, *A Wedding Story*, *Out In The Open*, *Tender*, *Behsharam (Shameless)* and *The Ramayana*.

Artistic Director **Jonathan Church**
Executive Director **Stuart Rogers**
Associate Director (Literary) **Ben Payne**

Box Office 0121 236 4455   Book online at www.birmingham-rep.co.uk

AUTHOR'S NOTE

I've been fascinated by prophets, revolutionaries and the trauma of violent social change, ever since I first read Norman Cohen's book *Pursuit of the Millennium* back in the 1960s. A fascination that intensified in the early seventies, when so many of my friends – if only for a time – became involved in revolutionary politics.

Through a Cloud isn't the first play I've written on this theme. It's intended as a companion play to *In Lambeth*, a play I wrote fifteen years ago, just before the Berlin Wall came down. It starts with the naked William Blake sitting in a tree with his equally naked wife, Kate, reading Milton's *Paradise Lost*.

The play centres around an argument between Blake and Tom Paine about the need for revolutionary change.

If *In Lambeth* is about the possibility of revolution, *Through a Cloud* is about its aftermath. The play is set in 1656, during the last years of the Commonwealth. Cromwell is a sick man. Milton is blind. The republic they have both helped to create is disintegrating, and together they pick their way through what's left of their broken dreams.

Both *In Lambeth* and *Through a Cloud* are concerned with the power of ideas, dreams, visions. Each play evolving around a passionate argument, in which the characters are defined, for the most part, through their beliefs.

Ideally what I'd like to do is write a play that goes between these two. A different sort of play. A narrative play, on an epic scale, teeming with wild characters, about the violence and confusion that revolution brings.

This would complete the picture, perhaps. A triptych, like one of those old altar pieces: figures in a landscape at either end, and a scene of chaos and devastation in the middle.

Jack Shepherd

THROUGH A CLOUD

Jack Shepherd

Cromwell, our chief of men, who through a cloud
Not by war only, but detractions rude,
Guided by faith and matchless fortitude,
To peace and truth thy glorious way hast ploughed . . .

From Milton's poem
'To the Lord General Cromwell'
May 1652

Characters

OLIVER CROMWELL (Noll), *late fifties. Two years before his death.*

JOHN MILTON, *late forties. Blind.*

KATHERINE WOODSTOCK, *twenty-seven years old. Tall. Fair hair.*

GEORGE GREEN, *an old man living wild.*

GUARD, *a non-speaking part.*

The play takes place in the woods surrounding Hampton Court Palace. The date is June 1656.

ACT ONE

Lights up to reveal a profusion of leaves. A tangle of trees: yew, holly, brambles, ivy. There are patches of long grass. Flowers. A stream lies just offstage.

Abundant. Verdant. Chaotic.

A figure pushes uncertainly through the undergrowth. His auburn hair is long. Only very slightly tinged with grey. His eyes unseeing. He carries a stick which he pushes forward in front of him.

JOHN. Are we there yet?

There is a woman just behind him. She's wearing a long white dress, untied and loosened at the neck, her hair tied up at the back.

KATHERINE. I don't think so.

He pushes awkwardly forward, swinging his stick. When he fails to make contact with anything, he stops.

JOHN. I don't understand. We *must* be there.

The woman emerges from the undergrowth. She is carrying a heavy wickerwork hamper.

KATHERINE. No we're not. I'm sorry. Not quite yet.

JOHN. You're sure?

She peers into the undergrowth.

KATHERINE. Yes.

Silence. He sits down heavily on the grass.

JOHN. Well I'll be damned.

KATHERINE. We should've stayed on the road.

JOHN. Nonsense.

She turns slightly away from JOHN, lifts the hem of her dress, pulls down her stocking and examines her leg.

KATHERINE. Anyway, we're lost now.

JOHN. No we're not. We're suffering a little delay in our inexorable progress forward. That's all.

KATHERINE. I've cut my knee.

JOHN. Oh dear. Oh dear. Oh dear. Have you cut it badly?

KATHERINE. No. It's just a scratch really. I fell over when we climbed the stile.

He moves closer to her.

JOHN. Is it deep?

KATHERINE. No, not very. It's nothing serious.

JOHN. Let me see.

He reaches out until he touches her leg. Then feels for the wound with the tip of his finger.

It's more than a scratch, I'm afraid.

He allows his hand to rest on her knee.

KATHERINE. It might be a sensible idea to bathe the wound in some water.

She lifts his hand from her knee, rapidly covering her legs with her dress.

A clean wound heals quicker. That's what my mother used to say.

JOHN. Then I'll fetch you some. There's a stream close by. I can hear it running.

KATHERINE. Thank you.

He stands.

Are you sure you can manage?

JOHN. Oh yes. Absolutely.

He searches for the hamper.

Isn't there a cup or something in the hamper?

She leads his hands to the hamper and he searches clumsily inside.

KATHERINE. It's just there.

He finds a cup. Cleans it out with his finger and then takes one or two paces in the direction of the stream.

And you're sure we're on the right track?

JOHN. Yes. Of course.

He stops.

I know exactly where I'm going. I always do.

He advances a few paces towards the stream, waving his stick in front of him.

It's something I pride myself on. And besides, I've been this way with Noll. On countless occasions in the past.

KATHERINE. Noll?

JOHN. Yes.

KATHERINE. I hope you're not going to call him that to his face.

He stops.

JOHN. And why not, for goodness' sake? Everyone else does.

KATHERINE. Well, I find it embarrassing. I mean, it sounds so presumptuous. 'Noll.' And not a little demeaning.

JOHN. I've told you before. He's not the ogre people imagine. You'll find him very affable, I promise you. Very approachable.

He takes a few more uncertain strides towards the stream.

And surprisingly solicitous, when he chooses to be. I mean, whenever we've come this way in the past, he's always been very careful to *describe* things for me. And in the most intricate detail. The pathways. The trees. The exact nature of the flowers, whenever we've come across them . . . Heart's Ease. Ragwort. Love-in-idleness.

A sudden flapping of wings from the undergrowth nearby.

The indistinct fluttering of a pheasant's wing, transformed through his prompting into the most colourful image of the thing itself.

KATHERINE. Well. If you'd paid a little less attention to nature, on these walks of yours . . . and a little more attention to the route, we wouldn't be in the pickle we're in now.

JOHN *swishes in front of him with his stick.*

JOHN. There's nothing particularly dangerous blocking my way, is there? Like a pit or a man-trap or whatever?

She stands and surveys his route.

KATHERINE. Not that I can see.

JOHN. Good.

He sets off warily in the direction of the stream. Holding his stick out in front of him

KATHERINE. And don't fall in!

JOHN. Don't you make a fuss! Just because I'm blind doesn't mean I'm totally incapacitated.

He disappears from view.

KATHERINE. And it's definitely a hut we're supposed to look out for? A gamekeeper's hut?

JOHN (*off*). That's right. It can't be very far away.

KATHERINE. And we're meeting him there about noon.

JOHN (*off*). Around noon. Yes. Though it wasn't a very *formal* arrangement, I hasten to add. As I remember it . . . the idea was to meet at the hut around lunch time . . . for an impromptu little *déjeuner* in the open air. That's all we agreed.

KATHERINE. I hope we've brought enough food.

JOHN *reappears, holding a cup of water.*

JOHN. It was his idea, actually. The whole thing. Thought it might free him from the *constrictions* of his present circumstances. Take him back to his days in the army, when life was altogether simpler. That's what he said, anyway.

He sets off towards her.

Between you and me, I don't think he enjoys Hampton Court. Rattling around in the sheer immensity of the place. Not his style really. Says he feels like a pea in a drum.

KATHERINE *laughs.*

Anyway, it'll give us a chance to talk things over. In a more informal setting, as it were. Just the pair of us. There's one or two things I need to try and straighten out.

He reaches out. Trying to establish where KATHERINE *is.*

Where are you?

KATHERINE. Here.

He sits down by her side.

I feel as if we're trespassing.

JOHN. Don't be so silly.

KATHERINE. I'm sorry, but I can't help feeling that we are! If we'd only come in through the main gate, then we could have introduced ourselves to the guards and told them we were on our way. And then at the very least . . . we'd be expected. But as it is, no one knows we're here. Not a soul.

He sits up and examines his breeches.

JOHN. I'm not sitting in anything I shouldn't be?

KATHERINE. No.

JOHN. Good.

He takes off his neckerchief and soaks it in the water.

KATHERINE. My mother always used to say that a trace of cobweb laid across the cut had very effective healing properties. Oh yes. And mouldy bread, too.

JOHN. How very bizarre. Now hold still. This might sting.

She modestly lifts her dress, exposing her wounded knee.

JOHN *reaches out and bathes the wound. It's an erotic image.* KATHERINE *sitting with her skirt unselfconsciously ruffled above her knees. And* JOHN, *lying on his stomach, glad of the opportunity to be this close to her, pressing his wet neckerchief against her bare leg.*

KATHERINE. Thank goodness for doctors. That's what I say. Last year I had a contagious flux of some sort, which our doctor considered rather serious. And so, during the course of the illness, he let out a quantity of blood each day. And believe it or not, six months later I was almost completely cured.

She examines the wound.

I think that's quite clean enough. Thank you.

She once more pushes down her dress.

JOHN. I love woods like these. Such dark smells. Full of old life. Fungus and toadstools. The feel of green lichen on the tree bark.

He rolls over in opportunistic fashion, resting his head on her lap and looking up towards her face with unseeing eyes.

Roots gripping the earth like the hands of giants. The crunch of pine cones underfoot. In such places it's easy to imagine the nymphs and dryads of the old mythology. Don't you think? Fawns lying by the river's edge, gazing lazily at passing dragonflies . . . That sort of thing. Water sprites swimming in the forest pools. Gentle zephyrs blowing through the trees.

He laughs.

And deep in the woods . . . the hairy-legged satyrs. With cloven feet and knees bent back like goats. Their bearded faces and upturned piggy noses thrusting through the undergrowth in search of ravishment.

The distant sound of a flute. KATHERINE *listens, unsure. It might just be her imagination.*

Greek culture was amazing, you know. The ancients knew everything. Absolutely everything. Eventually, of course, for reasons that are not entirely clear, their civilisation fell into ruin. And lay forgotten until quite recently in fact, when scholars started to realise – with something of a shock, I hasten to add – that this ancient culture knew an awful lot more about the arts and sciences . . . by which I mean the fabric . . . the very *mechanics* of our universe . . . than they did themselves.

KATHERINE. I wish I understood about mechanics.

JOHN. The question this poses, of course . . . is what on earth had happened to our progress – by which I mean *human* progress – in the intervening years?

Silence.

KATHERINE. Were they Christians . . . these Greeks?

JOHN. No.

Silence.

Unfortunately.

Silence.

KATHERINE. I feel so stupid sometimes.

JOHN. Oh, come now.

KATHERINE. Well, I do.

She disengages from him.

I don't really know about anything. Anything *important*, that is. I've never really had the chance.

JOHN. Keep faith, my love. Just a few more years of struggle. That's all that's needed. Life will be very different in the new Jerusalem. You mark my words.

Silence. He rings out the wet neckerchief and stuffs it in his pocket.

You're standing up.

KATHERINE. I am, yes. How can you tell?

JOHN. I sense things. (*Laughs.*) It's amazing when you lose one of your faculties how the others expand in compensation. I mean, just by being so close to you and – I don't know –

breathing the air around you. And from the merest touch of my fingers on your skin . . . I get a picture of you in my mind's eye as strong and as clear as if my sight had been miraculously returned.

KATHERINE. I'm glad to know your feelings for me are so heartfelt and so forceful, Mr Milton. But there is one slight thing that worries me . . .

JOHN. Go on.

KATHERINE. How does this image that you have of me, this picture of me that you say you are so in love with . . . how does this correspond to my real image? The person I am in the light of day? *Me* . . . that is to say.

JOHN. Sadly that is something I can never know. But I do love you, truly, nonetheless.

KATHERINE. John . . .

He takes her hand and pulls her down towards him.

We mustn't. Not yet a while. It would be wrong of us, quite wrong of us to betray our covenant with God.

They sit facing each other. Holding hands.

Once we're married . . . there'll be a time for dalliance and provocation. Until then I fear one's appetites are best kept on a leash.

JOHN. Perhaps.

He gets closer to her.

You see, in my view it's the intention to marry . . . the *commitment* that's important. Not the mere *act*. The ceremony itself. Such ritual is only the outward manifestation of a spiritual and timeless truth.

KATHERINE. Mmm.

JOHN. And that being so, we're free to do as we please.

She gently pushes his hands away.

KATHERINE. My father – God bless him – warned me about poets.

JOHN. Did he now?

KATHERINE. Yes. He said they were a bad lot, by and large. 'Idle. Self-centred. Scruffy. Carnal. And vain.'

JOHN. Solipsistic?

KATHERINE. Yes. That too, probably. It's an opinion pretty much shared by the whole family.

JOHN. Oh really?

KATHERINE. Yes, actually.

JOHN. But, I mean, if they all felt like that . . . how come they've all agreed to the wedding?

KATHERINE. They're prepared to make an exception in your case. Something to do with your reputation. Pathetic really, when you think about it.

JOHN. Is the cut healed on your leg?

He reaches out to touch it.

KATHERINE. It's only a scratch. I keep telling you.

She quickly pushes her dress down over her legs. His exploring hand finds the fabric. He runs his hands over the material.

JOHN. You must look wonderfully pretty in your new white dress. Framed by the exuberance . . . the luxuriance of nature, as it were. Like a painting in the French style. An allegorical work by . . . I don't know . . . Poussin perhaps.

He rests his head on her lap.

KATHERINE. I don't feel 'wonderfully pretty'. Not after that horrible journey in the carriage. I feel tired and hot. And I wish I'd come in more substantial shoes.

She sits up suddenly.

It would have made much more sense, you know . . . to have come in through the front gate

JOHN. Kate. Please.

KATHERINE. Well, it would. I mean, that's what he'll be
expecting us to do. What if he's had to go back to Whitehall
or something? And he's left a message at the gate?

JOHN. In all honesty, I don't think that's very likely, Kate.
I really don't. Not unless there's been some sort of
contingency that I don't know about.

KATHERINE. Well, there you are, then.

JOHN. As a general rule, he only travels to Whitehall during
the week.

*He impulsively kisses her shoulder. She moves away
slightly.*

Look, stop worrying. Everything's going to be all right.

KATHERINE. What if he's forgotten?

JOHN. I don't think so. We have a great deal to talk about.
The two of us. Though it's not the kind of thing I can
legitimately discuss with you, I'm afraid. Suffice it to say . . .
there's a decision to be made.

He kisses her on the cheek. His intentions now very clear.

KATHERINE. Decision? What sort of decision?

Silence.

JOHN. I'm sorry, but I can't tell you.

She holds him at arms length.

KATHERINE. It's a secret, then?

He nods.

You mustn't keep secrets from me.

She kisses him lightly and demurely on the cheek.

If as you say . . . John . . . we're man and wife already . . .
in all but name . . . then we shouldn't keep any secrets from
each other. I mean . . . would God want it otherwise?

JOHN. Very well, then . . . What vexes me is this . . .

He lowers his voice.

There are men within the Commonwealth, influential men
with an infectious and subversive voice . . . good men, too,
some of them . . . well-meaning men . . . not all bad . . .
who would have our dear old Noll, with his warts and his
temper and his long straggly hair, made king over us all.
They argue that he's king in all but name already, so why
not go the whole hog and have him king in actuality. King
Oliver Cromwell. Reigning alone and with absolute
authority. Aught else is sheer hypocrisy. Or so they claim.

KATHERINE. And you think it would be wrong of him to
accept such a role?

JOHN. I think it would be a disaster.

KATHERINE. You've never mentioned this before.

JOHN. I'm not yet in the habit of confiding in people, I'm
ashamed to say. Even those dearest to me. It would seem
not to be in my nature.

KATHERINE. Don't bite my head off for saying this . . . but
there's people in my family of the opinion that with a king
back on the throne, we'd get back to a bit of peace and
quiet. The way it was meant to be.

JOHN. Oh really? 'Meant to be'? What are you talking about?
'Meant to be'? For seven years . . .

KATHERINE. John . . .

JOHN. For seven years . . . near enough . . . We've been a free
people, have we not? Free to govern our country as we, the
nation, see fit. What do you want us to do? Put our necks
back into the yoke and meekly surrender all our authority,
won at such terrible cost, to the arbitrary dominance of a
single individual?

KATHERINE. John. It's not –

JOHN. Our last King went to the block. Tyranny died with
him. Or so we all believed.

KATHERINE. It's not *my* opinion, John. It's my family. I'm
just repeating what people've said.

JOHN. Do you – oh, all right, then – *they* – Do *they* want to see all that unravelled? Oppression welcomed back into the fold? And thereby have us lose . . . through a lack of nerve . . . faith . . . vision . . . *and* I might add . . . the necessary bloody-mindedness – all the battles we have won? 'Ye shall cry out on that day because of the king that ye have chosen, and the Lord will not hear you in that day.' First Book of Samuel, Chapter 8, Verse 18.

KATHERINE. But does it not say in Isaiah: 'Behold, a king shall reign in righteousness. And princes shall in sit in judgement'?

JOHN. It does indeed. But the Book of Isaiah also tells us. In Chapter 33, I think . . . Verse 22. Or thereabouts. 'The Lord is our judge . . . our lawgiver . . . The Lord is our king.'

Silence.

Your knowledge of the Bible is surprisingly good. Especially for a woman. I though you told me your father didn't want you reading the Old Testament. That he positively discouraged you.

KATHERINE. Yes. That's true. He did. There were certain parts of it he didn't think girls should look at.

JOHN. And which parts were those?

KATHERINE. Do I have to spell it out?

JOHN. You mean . . . David spying on Bathsheba in her nakedness . . . that sort of thing?

KATHERINE. Yes. That's exactly what I mean. He also said I'd find a lot of it boring, which I did, of course. But it didn't put me off.

JOHN. And what did you make of 'The Song of Solomon'? 'The Song of Songs'?

Silence.

'Thy lips *are* like a thread of scarlet, and thy speech *is* comely; thy temples *are* like a piece of a pomegranate within thy locks.'

He kisses her sensuously on the forehead.

Why 'pomegranate', I always thought.

KATHERINE. Mr Milton. You are incorrigible.

JOHN. In our household . . . problematic pages like these had been rather untactfully torn out.

He kisses her on the lips. The kiss becomes more intense.
JOHN *pulls* KATHERINE *gently downward so that they both lie together on the ground.*

The sound of the flute. Closer this time.

JOHN *lies on top of* KATHERINE. *Kissing her neck. The flute stops. And the bushes wave about as though in a wind. And then a face pushes through. Old. Bearded. Surrounded by foliage. The face of a satyr. Leaves seem to be issuing from his mouth.*

KATHERINE *sees the face and stifles a scream.*

KATHERINE. Oh my God! What's that? Oh God.

The face withdraws.

JOHN. What is it? What's the matter?

KATHERINE. I saw a face.

She gets up in a panic. Backing away from where she saw the face.

JOHN. Nonsense.

KATHERINE. No. Not nonsense, I did! A human face. But also an animal's . . . Like one of those . . . I don't know . . . hairy-legged things you were describing. A goat maybe. Or even a pig.

JOHN. It was your imagination. A trick of the light.

KATHERINE. No. No. No. It was *real*!

He gets to his feet and walks uncertainly towards her.

JOHN. Where are you exactly?

KATHERINE. I'm *here*. Come on. Take my hand.

She reaches out to him and he takes her hand.

JOHN. A forest can have a very profound effect on people.

He tries to embrace her.

It can talk to us – as it were – with an ancient voice. As if a memory of the old religion is held by magic in the very bark.

She pushes him away.

KATHERINE. I know what I saw.

JOHN. Yes. Dearest. But I didn't.

KATHERINE. Well, that's hardly surprising, is it?

JOHN. True. But the fact remains that nothing whatever impinged on my surviving senses, which – need I remind you – are very finely tuned.

KATHERINE. You had other things on your mind. Come on. Let's go. For pity's sake.

They leave the way they came.

(*Off.*) And please let me lead the way this time.

Silence.

A near-naked figure runs out from the undergrowth. He drops down beside the stream and scoops up handfuls of water into his mouth. Though he still wears the ragged remnants of a shirt and breeches, he has the look of one of Poussin's woodland creatures. There is a small wooden flute hanging by a frayed cord from his neck. He plays a phrase on it. Not unlike bird song.

Silence.

He sees the hamper. Runs over to it. Pushes his hand inside and pulls out a knife, testing the edge of it with his thumb. He sniffs the contents and then seizes a large pear from deep inside.

MAN (*muttering*). I thank thee, oh pear tree, for thy bounty. That through the sacrifice of thy fruit, I might survive for one more day.

He looks at the pear. And then sings very quietly. Almost tunelessly.

God is in the pear tree.
Yet it won't ever grow.
If I eat the so-and-so.

He cuts off the stem and then devours it hungrily.

But all's not lost.
No. No. Not a bit.
For God makes the seed to grow . . .
Out of my shit.

He sticks the knife into the ragged remnants of his waistband. Puts the flute to his mouth and elaborates on the tune. He stops suddenly.

Oh bugger. They're coming back.

He plunges into the undergrowth and lies still. The stage is empty for a while.

JOHN (*off*). Why have we stopped?

KATHERINE (*off*). We've come round in a circle.

JOHN appears, hands stretched out in front of him. He stops. KATHERINE pushes past.

JOHN. Impossible.

KATHERINE. No. It's true. Look. There's the hamper we left behind.

JOHN. Where? Show me.

She leads him to the hamper. His hand explores the surface of the hamper.

Are you certain it's ours?

KATHERINE. I'm positive. I packed it myself.

She examines the contents.

Strange . . . I'm sure I put in more fruit . . . Anyway. We should've definitely gone over the stile.

JOHN. No.

KATHERINE. I could swear I saw a chimney through the trees.

JOHN. You were looking in the wrong direction.

KATHERINE. How can you be so sure?

JOHN. I had an image in my mind of the way we ought to take. And insofar as I am able to remember, it did not concur with yours.

KATHERINE. Don't be ridiculous. We should've gone over the stile. That had to be the way. Absolutely had to. Over the stile. And then on past the big oak tree. I mean, there was a path on the other side, for heaven's sake.

JOHN. No. I don't think so.

KATHERINE. In your condit – I mean, you can't even – God's truth. You're so opinionated. There's no room in your heart for even the slightest disagreement.

JOHN. No.

KATHERINE. Think hard, John. Is there no possibility that you might be wrong . . . in this matter?

JOHN. No possibility whatsoever.

KATHERINE. I mean, if we can't agree about this . . . what's going to happen when we disagree about something important? Like the house we're going to live in? Or the education of our children?

Silence.

Do you honestly expect me to go along with you in everything . . . John? Even when you're clearly in the wrong?

JOHN. Have you quite finished?

Silence.

Good. Well, let me just say this. I'm by no means an unreasonable man. If you think you know a better way to the house, then fine . . . by all means, take it.

KATHERINE. John . . . !

JOHN. Take it. Go on. But don't expect me to come with you.

KATHERINE. John. That's not the –

JOHN. You're free to go in any direction you want. North. South. East or west. I'm not going to stop you. Off you go.

Silence.

And if you happen to end up in the farmyard of some enraged farmer, as I honestly suspect you will, up to your knees in muck and swill . . . on your head be it. But don't come crawling back to me, in a state of the most abject apology, pleading with me to give you the proper directions, because in all probability, I won't be here. I'll be waiting for you at the appointed place, sharing a glass of wine with our host, lying in the shade, I shouldn't wonder, in a state of the uttermost contentment.

KATHERINE. You're impossible.

And she goes. Long silence.

(*Off.*) I'll come back for you! Don't worry. Just stay where you are! I won't be very long!

He spins round, trying to get his bearings.

JOHN. Take as long as you like! I don't care. I can manage perfectly well on my own, thank you very much. I know exactly what I'm doing!

He walks forward a few paces. Arms outstretched until he collides with a tree. He sits down. His head in his hands. Rocking slightly. Singing a psalm to himself.

That man hath perfect blessedness
Who walketh not astray.
In counsel of ungodly men,
Nor stands in sinners' way.

Nor sitteth in the scorner's chair
But placeth his delight
Upon God's law and meditates
On his law day and night.

He is joined by the voice of a MAN *from the bushes.* JOHN *stops singing, listening in some alarm.*

MAN.

> He shall be like a tree that grows
> Near planted by a river,
> Which in his season yields his fruit
> And his leaf fadeth never.

JOHN. Who was that?

The sound of the flute, clumsily picking out the tune.

MAN. Me. It was me, sir.

The MAN *pushes his way to the edge of the undergrowth and stands there, only partly visible.*

I hope you didn't mind me joining in. I haven't heard a good psalm in ever such a long while. I do like a good psalm.

He plays again.

Yeah. I seen you here a short while ago. With your good lady. And then when the both of you pushed off, I spotted you gone off without your hamper. So I took the liberty of helping myself to a pear. I didn't mean no harm by it. I was just hungry. And a very good pear it was too. If you don't mind me saying so.

JOHN. You have me at a disadvantage, sir. I'm entirely at your mercy. And demonstrably quite defenceless. I trust you're not sufficiently desperate to want to take advantage of a blind man.

MAN. You blind?

JOHN. Yes. Utterly. Unequivocally.

The MAN *briefly sticks his head out of the bushes and peers intently at* JOHN.

MAN. You don't look blind.

JOHN. No. Appearances can be deceptive.

MAN. So people say.

Silence.

JOHN. It wouldn't be very prudent to assault me, by the way.
I don't have any money about my person. I'm very well
connected. And I'm also terribly well known. Not just in
this country, I might add. And so, in consequence . . . were
you in any way to 'lay into me', as it were . . . I'm sure the
repercussions would be simply awful.

MAN. What's your name, then?

JOHN. John Milton.

MAN. Is that so?

Silence.

Mine's George Green.

JOHN. Pleased to meet you, George.

GEORGE. Likewise, I'm sure. What do you say we have a
little dig around in that hamper of yours?

JOHN. No.

GEORGE *comes out of the undergrowth. Snatches another
pear out of the hamper. And once he's sure that* JOHN
hasn't noticed, he sits down under the tree JOHN *is leaning
against, and starts eating it as quietly as he can.*

My wife brought it . . . to sustain us on our outing. Well,
she isn't my wife yet . . . quite . . . but she very soon will be.
And she'd be most upset if I shared it with anyone. However
needy they might actually prove to be.

GEORGE. Mmm. Strange, isn't it . . . how everything we eat
has been alive at one time. Not possible to eat the stones.
Or the dead things. Like copper. Or tin. No sustenance in
them. See. For something to be nourishing it has to have
lived. And then, of course, died. One life sacrificed that
another might thrive.

Silence.

It's God, of course . . . working his wondrous purpose in
every living thing and fellow creature. I know this because
God is in me. God is within.

He wipes his mouth on his sleeve.

Not *just* me, I hasten to add. I'd be mad to think that. He's everywhere. In the leaves of the trees up there. And in the air that's between them. He's in the branches and the roots. The earth, too. He's in that. And the worms underneath the earth. The tools you dig with. The shovel and the wheelbarrow. And when you get back home, he's in the kitchen. The stove and the cooking pot. He's even in the sideboard and the cupboard where you hang your coat.

JOHN. Oh really?

GEORGE. Yes. This explains the order that's in everything. The balance. Don't you see? The harmony all around us. It's what makes our lives predictable. Bearable, I should say . . . I mean, if God *wasn't* inside everything, there'd be chaos, wouldn't there? You'd wake up in the morning and everything would be gone. Or much too big. Or too little. Just imagine it, eh? Too . . . *little*. Or sort of flying off at angles and disappearing down holes. Sheer chaos, Mr Milton. Stands to reason.

JOHN. Are you a Ranter?

GEORGE. I was at one time . . . of the Ranting Fraternity. Yes. But not any more. Though between you and me . . . I still think they got a point.

JOHN. You're eating one of our pears.

GEORGE. No. I just dribble a lot. It's the fresh air . . . Gives me an appetite all the time.

JOHN. So people say.

Silence.

GEORGE. I was with Clarkson in '49. At the height of his powers he was, then. Ranting up and down the country. Preaching in the open air. Praising God in the alehouses.

JOHN. Yes. I've heard it said you met in the alehouses.

GEORGE. That's right. To sing psalms. To drink the holy sacrament of the ale. To suck on a pipe full of tobacco. Each of us in turn pulling on the sacramental weed. They were good days, Mr Milton. Heady days. Before the magistrates put a stop to it all.

He laughs suddenly.

Fucking with Mrs Simcock and Mrs Prothero on the floor of The Lamb and Flag in Dymchurch. Bodies rolling in the fireplace. Hands reaching under dresses to the glory of the Lord. Oh yes, Mr Milton . . . They were good old days indeed.

JOHN. And never to come again?

GEORGE. No. I don't think so. Not in my lifetime. Mr Cromwell don't like Ranters. It's not allowed any more.

JOHN. I see.

GEORGE. Most of our lot went to prison, Mr Milton. So did I for a time. They'd only release us if we promised to be quiet and join the Quakers. Which was a bit of a mockery, if you ask me. Peacocks trying to be reptiles. Crawling under stones.

JOHN. Not for you, eh?

GEORGE. No. Not for me. (*Taps nose.*) I went my own way.

JOHN. Evidently.

Silence.

GEORGE. So what you doing here? In this here neck of the woods? Bit off the beaten track, aren't you? I mean, if you've come to see Mr Cromwell, you'd've done better to've come in by the gate.

JOHN. True. I had a little altercation with my wife – or rather my wife to be – on that very subject, only a short while ago.

GEORGE. I know. I heard.

Silence.

Friend of yours, is he?

JOHN. Who, Cromwell?

GEORGE. Who else?

JOHN. Not a friend exactly. Not that we're . . . More of a colleague, really.

GEORGE. Oh yes?

JOHN. Yes. I have a Parliamentary position, you see . . .
Secretary for Foreign Languages . . . Not as imposing as it
sounds, actually. Rather humdrum if anything. Translating
documents into Latin. And Italian on occasions . . . That
sort of thing.

GEORGE. Can't be easy without eyes.

JOHN. The problems are not insurmountable. With the aid of
a responsive amanuensis.

Silence.

GEORGE. Bit out of your element, though . . . ain't you?
Wandering about in these here woods?

JOHN. I wouldn't say that exactly.

GEORGE. A little termite thingummy come crawling out of
its mound. Easy for someone to step on you and not know
they done it. What I'm saying . . . There ain't no 'Protec-
torate' operating out here. No chance, mate. Out here in the
wild we live by different rules. 'Dog eat dog.' That's what
they say in the big city, ain't it? But in these here woods it's
altogether more natural. More a case of 'snake eat bird'.

JOHN. That's a very startling concept. Would you care to
expound a little?

GEORGE. 'Expound'?

JOHN. Yes. If you'd care to.

GEORGE. It's not often I'm asked to '*expound*', it's 'Shut
your face and keep your nose clean' mainly. All I'm saying,
Mr Milton . . . life in these here woods might seem a bit
harsh to the outsider . . . like yourself . . . everything
feeding off everything else . . . but for us who live here . . .
it's the natural way of things.

JOHN. In what sense 'natural'?

GEORGE. A Garden of Eden . . . Mr Milton . . . but after the
serpent's crawled in.

JOHN. I see.

GEORGE. There's more than just me, you know. Living wild. Scratching out a living. Here and there. Nowhere we can call home. There's a whole army of us, actually. Roaming the land. Lepers and murderers. Them as didn't come out right in the wash. Yeah. And nutters too. (*Laughs.*) There's no need to look so surprised. I mean, when you think about it, we have to go *somewhere*, don't we? We can't just disappear. We're not going to be swallowed up in the earth just for the convenience of good people like yourself. Or troop off into Hell.

JOHN. I don't believe in Hell.

GEORGE. On the contrary, Mr Milton . . . I do believe in Hell. Because Hell is here on earth.

JOHN. I wouldn't dispute that.

A horn sounds. KATHERINE's voice shouting: 'John! Where are you? John!'

GEORGE. That be you missus, I expect.

JOHN. Yes. She went to find Noll. Oliver. You know . . . The Lord Protector. They'll be on their way back . . . with guards, I shouldn't wonder.

GEORGE. Cromwell, eh?

He takes out the knife.

JOHN. That's right.

Distant shouting. OLIVER's voice, indistinct: 'You take the path. I'll go round by the yew wood.'

GEORGE. I ain't always been like this, you know. I was proper once. Lived a life as good as any man. Until they came along.

JOHN. Who? Until who came along exactly?

GEORGE. The Parliamentary hordes, Mr Milton. With Cromwell at their head. Descending on our village like a plague of locusts from the Bible's darker pages. This were back in '43, you understand. When the war were at its height.

Sharp whistles. OLIVER *calling out indistinctly. 'Keep 'em on a leash man! Keep 'em on a leash!'*

JOHN. What happened?

GEORGE. Fire and ashes, Mr Milton. Ruin and desolation. Beyond any possible justification! Like splinters in the brain. Slivers of broken glass jammed into the living skull.

He holds his head.

I mean, is it any wonder I started thinking God were mad? And sent the world out of kilter. And even now . . . Sometimes . . . in my quiet moments . . . when I reach inside, I can feel his disturbance in here. In the disquiet of my own spirit, I get an echo of a deeper, more universal disquiet. A fluxious distemper of the brain pan.

He scampers up a tree.

JOHN. What was done to you, man? What in God's name was done to you? And by whom?

GEORGE. There's one man to blame. And one man only. One face in a sea of upturned pious faces. Eclipsing all the others. With reddened eyes and sackcloth of hair. Emanating malignancy. Peering through smoke and sulphur. A great head of brass and of steel. Mightier than Azazel. More terrible in his wrath than Samael, Dagon, Moloch and all the teeming hordes of Gehenna's plain.

A woman's voice calls out: 'John! John!'

JOHN. Who in heaven's name?

GEORGE. That man there!

A loud blast of horns. Much closer this time and OLIVER *bursts through the undergrowth. Sweating and out of breath.*

OLIVER. You again. You madman!

KATHERINE *follows* OLIVER *out of the undergrowth.*

KATHERINE. John. Thank God you're all right.

She embraces him.

OLIVER. I've told you before about trespassing on my property. I've borne all your annoyance as patiently as I am able. And God only knows I am a patient man. But your constant harassment, sir . . . your sheer pestiferousness is beyond annoyance. It's tantamount to persecution!

KATHERINE. I'm sorry. So sorry.

She holds JOHN *protectively.*

OLIVER. And not content with making my life a misery, you're now badgering my friends and colleagues with your impertinence and delusions and your vile nakedness! I've had enough of it! Do you hear me? I've had enough of it, sir!

KATHERINE. My poor dear. I should never have abandoned you. It was wrong of me. Please please forgive me.

JOHN. Don't fuss.

GEORGE. Get too close, Cromwell, and I'll shit all over you.

KATHERINE *looks up. Startled to see* GEORGE *in the tree.*

OLIVER. He would too.

He backs away slightly.

GEORGE. Better be making tracks.

GEORGE *leaps down from the tree. He growls at* OLIVER *like an animal.*

KATHERINE. His was the face I saw.

JOHN. What?

KATHERINE. Just now. Peering through the bushes. Glaring at me like an animal. His was the face.

GEORGE. It's a rotten tree that taints the forest!

He circles around OLIVER, *brandishing the knife.*

OLIVER. That's enough.

GEORGE. Such rottenness has to be cut away, Mr Milton! Cut away with axes of iron and saws of brass! Or the woods of the world will perish! And the Tree of Life itself will lose its crown of leaves!

OLIVER. Enough! Do you hear? Enough! Enough! *Enough!*

GEORGE *scurries away into the undergrowth in a totally unexpected direction.*

Any more of this and I'll summon the Master of Hounds and have you hunted down like an animal! I'll gorge my dogs on your bloody carcass! And see your wrinkled pelt nailed to a tree with the crows and the vermin! Do you hear?

OLIVER *rushes after him. Lashing at the bushes with his stick.*

KATHERINE. It's all my fault. It was a sin to leave you like that. Oh yes it was, John. A sin. You must have been so frightened?

JOHN. No, my love. Not really. Since most people, these days, have me at an advantage. It's far better to trust them, I find, than than to slink around like a beaten dog always fearing the worst.

OLIVER (*off*). Get after him! What are you waiting for? *After* him, you useless tubs of lard.

The barking of dogs.

KATHERINE. I'm so sorry, John.

JOHN. There's no need to be sorry. We had an honest disagreement. That's all. Why muddy things up with compromise and apology?

OLIVER (*off*). I don't care what your orders are! Get after him. I'm not a child! I can take care of myself.

KATHERINE. I found the hut, by the way. He was waiting for us at the hut.

JOHN. How very fortunate.

The yelping of the dogs starts to fade as GEORGE *is pursued deeper into the forest.*

KATHERINE. Yes. It's only a little way up the track. If we'd gone on just a bit further . . . we'd've got there without any difficulty.

JOHN. Yes. Well, I knew it couldn't be very far.

OLIVER *emerges from the undergrowth. Eyes shut. Holding his head.*

OLIVER. Can't seem to get my breath.

He's in a bad way. Red in the face. Sweating. Dizzy. Weak-kneed, unsure of what he's seeing.

KATHERINE. Whatever's the matter?

OLIVER. You ever seen a ship's hawser tightening round a capstan?

KATHERINE *shakes her head.*

Well, that's what it feels like. In here. And my old head's fit to burst with the all the pressure that's inside.

KATHERINE. You poor thing.

OLIVER. And I can't hear nothing. Not distinctly. Just a roaring in my ears . . . like the sea.

She runs to OLIVER *and tries to steady him.*

JOHN. What's happening?

KATHERINE. He's not well, John. Not well at all.

OLIVER. Just give me a moment. It'll pass.

KATHERINE. Lean on me. Go on. I can bear your weight. That's it . . . Now try and sit yourself down.

She sits him down.

And rest your back against this tree.

OLIVER. Thank you. Thank you kindly.

KATHERINE *briefly lays a hand on his forehead.*

If my men could see me now . . . eh? Unable to sit down without a slip of a girl to help me . . . they'd laugh themselves fit to burst.

Silence.

Doesn't do to quarrel, John. Our Lord spoke agin it. And besides . . . it ain't safe out here on your own. Not with your eyesight. The land is rife with desperate men.

KATHERINE. He's too hot.

OLIVER. Yes. Too hot. Yes.

The rustle of branches betrays the presence of the guards.

In case you're wondering, my men-at-arms will not be very far away. They're not supposed to leave me unattended at any time. Though I always tell them to be discreet about it. And not come barging in unnecessarily.

KATHERINE. John . . . Could you bring me some water from the stream? Like you did before?

JOHN. Yes. Of course. Glad to be of assistance. Have we anything . . . Sufficiently capacious . . . as it were . . . to contain the necessary liquid?

KATHERINE. I'm sure I put a bowl in the hamper. Use that.

OLIVER. I get too angry. That's what does it.

KATHERINE. Hush now.

OLIVER. In days gone by I could fly off the handle . . . and not think twice about it . . . But these days . . . it near drains the life out of me.

JOHN. Where's the hamper?

KATHERINE. Just in front of your nose.

OLIVER. I know the Lord wants me to keep to the straight and narrow path . . . But certain people, I'm afraid . . . drive me beyond the bounds of faith and reason.

JOHN *finds the hamper and scrabbles around inside it.*

And so, whenever I have the misfortune to set eyes on that madman . . . that pestilential loon . . . flaunting his nakedness . . . and disseminating his foul subversions . . . I tell you . . .

JOHN. I can't find a bowl.

KATHERINE. Then use a cup. Like you did before. Hurry.

OLIVER. I tell you . . . My blood begins to boil.

JOHN *picks up a cup. And then, arms outstretched in front of him, he feels his way towards the stream.*

JOHN. I am going the right way?

KATHERINE. Yes. Just keep going forward.

JOHN (*muttering*). Only the heady excitements of the last few
  moments seem to have temporarily disrupted my usually
  infallible sense of my own whereabouts.

He stumbles into the undergrowth.

OLIVER. What it is, you see . . . he holds me responsible,
  personally responsible for a wrong once done to him.
  A crime he claims was committed just after the outbreak
  of the Civil War. '42. Or '43. Can't remember exactly. Up in
  the Lincolnshire Fens somewhere.

KATHERINE. Hurry up with that water, John.

OLIVER. At that time, you see . . . he was a wood-carver.
  Known and respected throughout the county. And what he'd
  done, he'd restored the icons in a little village church up
  there. Deeping St Ann, I think they call it. Took him the
  best part of a lifetime. But when some of my men, who
  happened to be billeted in the village, took exception to
  these carvings and righteously hacked them out of the body
  of the church . . . he lost his wits, poor chap. And went
  wild-wood mad.

*JOHN returns with a cup full of fresh water. He concentrates
so hard on not spilling any of the water that he loses his
bearings again.*

JOHN. Where are you?

KATHERINE. Over here.

OLIVER. All this is, of course, perfectly comprehensible in
  the context of such unprecedented civil disturbance. But the
  blame . . . the *culpability*, which is then attached to me
  personally, for this desperate and perhaps over-zealous
  act . . . is neither reasonable nor is it tolerable . . . I'm afraid
  to say –

He struggles to get his breath.

– since I was fifty miles away at the time, raising a
  company of horse.

JOHN. Over-zealous?

OLIVER. Yes. These were good men, you understand. Salt of the earth. Trust them with my life. And though I am unwilling to censure them for what they did . . . I find I cannot condone them either. Not entirely.

JOHN. And where does that leave you exactly?

OLIVER. Seeking out the truth that lies in my heart. And in the heart of every man.

JOHN *gets closer to* KATHERINE *and carefully passes her the cup of water.*

KATHERINE. Shush. Shush. There's no need to excite yourself.

OLIVER. And so the wretched man pursues me, seeking recompense for his deep sense of grievance. Cajoling me. Harassing me into making amends. And always at a distance, the crafty devil. Just out of reach. Try as I might, I just can't seem to lay a hand on him.

KATHERINE *helps him into an upright position.*

And then, of course, when he falls in with Clarkson and the Ranting Fraternity, their damned nonsense gets right under his skin and makes him even worse.

KATHERINE. They do smoke an awful lot of tobacco. Or so I'm told.

She gives him a drink of water.

OLIVER. Sometimes I see him on the Embankment, throwing horse shite at my barge as it passes. Or he's waiting in the street outside Whitehall, shouting his demented slogans through my carriage window. And at weekends sometimes, he wakes me in the night, hollering in the trees below. But he's never been as bold as this before. Never come as close. (*Tearful.*) In my darker moments . . . I see him as a spectre born out of my own despair . . . Sprung shrieking out of the top of my head . . . to taunt me for all the mistakes I've made . . . the sins I've committed . . . the promises I've broken. And all our shattered dreams.

KATHERINE. I need something for a compress.

JOHN. Here. Use this.

He takes the damp and bloodstained scarf from his pocket and hands it to KATHERINE.

Take heart, comrade. We may have taken a few hard knocks in the past six years or so. But the fight goes on. We're not finished yet. Not by any manner of means. The 'good old cause' will still prevail.

Silence. KATHERINE *dips the scarf in the water. Squeezes out the excess and applies a cold compress to* OLIVER*'s brow.*

OLIVER. Thank you. That's very agreeable.

KATHERINE. It'll draw the heat out of you . . . as my old mother used to say.

OLIVER. Did she? Did she really?

KATHERINE. Yes. She nursed me back to health many times.

OLIVER. They say my mother's . . . common . . . you know . . . Simple reason that she don't know how to behave in polite company . . . But she's a treasure . . . A paragon of Christian virtue . . . How dare they say such things . . . ?

KATHERINE. Shhh. Shhh. Shhh. Close your eyes. Rest for a moment. Get your strength back.

OLIVER. How dare they?

OLIVER *lies back. Shutting his eyes.*

KATHERINE (*whispered*). His sweat's not right, John. Smells of gunpowder. He's not well at all.

The distant sound of a hunting horn. The yapping of dogs.

OLIVER. Damned scoundrel's getting away.

KATHERINE. There there. It's all right.

JOHN. He may well be mad, that I'll grant you. But the man's no scoundrel, not as far as I can see.

OLIVER. No? You're lucky to be alive, John Milton. I'm telling you. A couple more minutes and he'd've slit your throat and stripped the clothes off your back.

KATHERINE. Sh . . . Sh . . . Sh . . . Lie still.

She presses the compress against his brow.

OLIVER. Just because he says he believes in God doesn't mean you can *trust* him, you know. Same with all these damn Ranters. It's not a 'belief' at all, in fact, in my humble opinion. It's a disease. An infection. Once it gets into the system, it courses through the body like a poison. Inflames a man's opinion of himself . . . until he's higher – in his own estimation – than God in Majesty. With no proper respect for property. None at all. And blind to people's basic needs. Same with the Anabaptists. Fifth Monarchists. Diggers. Levellers. Muggletonians. Aye. And all the rest of them. They're all tarred with the same brush. You couldn't make me another compress, could you? My head's on fire.

He hands the scarf to KATHERINE, *who soaks it once more in the water.*

JOHN (*carefully*). It's important, though, that we let them be, don't you think?

KATHERINE. John.

He motions for her to be quiet.

JOHN. Live alongside them. Try and come to terms with their needs. Yes, even the most dangerous of them. Unless, of course, they're threatening the very fabric of the state. You see, there's a principle at stake here: a man must have the right to worship God in whatsoever way he chooses.

OLIVER. Yes. Yes. Yes. I know . . .

KATHERINE *reapplies the compress.*

JOHN. It's why we fought the war, for heaven's sake.

OLIVER. I know. I know that. But when a man –

JOHN. At least why I –

OLIVER. When a man starts to lay claim to another man's property. And when his beliefs and practices start to interfere with the good order and the proper administration of the country . . . then the limits of toleration have been reached. And something has to be done.

He sits up suddenly, throwing off the compress.

It must be what God wants of us. Order. Decency. Harmony. Of that I've always been sure. It can't. It just can't be otherwise. Is that a wine bottle I can see in that hamper of yours? A sip or two would cheer me up no end.

JOHN. Yes, it is actually. Elderberry wine. I'll get you a glass. If you think it'll do you some good.

KATHERINE. No, John . . . You stay where you are. I'll do it.

She goes to the hamper and takes out an opened bottle of red wine, which she pours into a small glass and then carefully hands to OLIVER.

JOHN. It's an awful contradiction though, isn't it? The rights of the individual set against the needs of the country as a whole. I mean, if our Commonwealth is to stay healthy, both have to be respected. Anarchy lies in one direction. Tyranny in the other. Somehow we have to steer a middle course, wouldn't you say? And not look back. No matter how tempting it might be to do so.

KATHERINE. Don't drink it too fast.

OLIVER. Good for the blood . . . as my doctor tells me.

He takes a sip of wine.

I know you think we should go easy on these sectaries, John. These extremists. Allow them to breathe and so forth. Show them a little toleration. And you're right. In an ideal society that's exactly what our attitude should be. But things are far from perfect in this Commonwealth of ours . . . as we both know only too well. The balance of . . . *things* . . . is very delicate . . . and it wouldn't take much to throw us out of kilter and turn the world on its head again. Everywhere you look there are people doing their damnedest to bring this regime of ours to a bloody and abrupt end.

He gulps down more wine.

There's Royalists in every country house. On every street
corner . . . in constant communication with the King over
the water – or so Thurloe tells me – sitting there in Bruges
with 'seven thousand and eight hundred men', just waiting
for the word. There's priests in hiding. Jesuits under every
bed. And then, of course, there's the sectarian minority
who'd deal with the devil himself if they thought it would
see the back of me. And bring them one step closer to
realising their fanatic dreams of a new social order. So you
see. We're not safe. Not safe at all.

He wipes the sweat out of his eyes with his sleeve.

Seems quite random, doesn't it? At first glance. All these . . .
things . . . apparently disconnected . . . one from the other.
But once you realise it's the King of Spain who's behind it
all, then everything starts to slip into place.

*He reaches for the wine bottle and pours himself another
glass.*

He's the thread that connects them all together. Charles
Stuart. Papists. Ranters. All the aforementioned forces in
fact, threatening the very existence of our state. He's the
power that gives the shadow of conspiracy both force and
substance. He pulls a string in Madrid. And next thing you
know there's an insurrection breaking out in Buckingham-
shire. Or someone who should know better is sailing off to
Spain, promising him friendly anchorage, when the time
comes to invade. Make no mistake, Mr Milton. The
Spaniolisation of Albion is well under way!

Silence.

JOHN. Whilst conceding that much of what you say is true,
I can't escape the conclusion that your feverous state is
beginning to affect your judgement somewhat. And your
customarily sanguine nature is being overwhelmed by
vapours of a melancholic sort.

Silence.

OLIVER. I'm as right as I'll ever be.

KATHERINE *picks up the discarded scarf and wrings it out.*

When you get to my age, Mr Milton . . . it's hard enough just staying alive.

KATHERINE. Your scarf's still wet I'm afraid, John. Shall I spread it out in the sunlight? It'll be dry in no time.

JOHN. No. Don't bother. I'll wear it as it is.

KATHERINE. You'll get a stiff neck.

JOHN. I wouldn't worry about that.

He puts it back on.

There's many would say I'm stiff-necked enough already. Isn't that so, Mr Cromwell?

OLIVER. True enough. Yes. Though perhaps something of an understatement.

He stands up with difficulty.

Thank you for all your . . . ministrations . . . Katherine. But I'm feeling a little stronger now. The crisis would seem to be over. For the time being at least.

He walks around. Tries to improve the flow of blood to his feet by stamping on the grass.

I dutifully consume all the medicines the quack prescribes for me. But I can't say I feel any the better for it. Worse if anything. And whenever I complain about it, he tells me that he has to be cruel in order to be kind. Or some such homely nonsense. And on we go with the treatments.

KATHERINE. What's the matter with you? Do the doctors know?

OLIVER. It's old age mainly, I suppose, whatever the doctors say. The slow mortification of the vitals. Comes to us all in the end. Though I do suffer from time to time with a recurring fever. Been troubled with it for years. Leaves me prostrate for a few days. And then it goes away again.

JOHN. You're not suffering from it now?

OLIVER. No. No. No. I fear my present woes are something else entirely.

Awkward silence.

KATHERINE. Shall I lay out the food?

OLIVER. Yes. By all means. Always enjoyed eating in the open air. Though I don't get hungry these days. Not like I used to.

> KATHERINE *starts unpacking the hamper and laying the contents on the grass. Wine. Cheese. Ham. Bread. Plates. Knives. Beakers. Napkins.*

KATHERINE. Happiness is so short-lived, isn't it? And so is misery, thank goodness. If you're sad one day, it doesn't mean to say you won't be happy the next. Yesterday, down by the river, I saw a kingfisher perched on a pole. Its feathers were still wet from skimming over the water and diving down for fish. Such a beautiful bird. I wanted to hold it. Feel its beating heart. But when I got too close, it flew away in a dazzle of blue.

She lays three places on the grass. Each one with plate, knife, beaker and napkin.

What makes us so special, Mr Cromwell? Who's to say the birds and the animals don't feel just like we do. And the insects too . . . Joy. Hunger. Hope and despair. Who's to say?

Silence.

When I was a little girl, I was told by our minister that animals didn't have souls. That only *we* have souls, we humans. And it upset me terribly. Aren't they mortal, too, I thought, just like we are? What makes us so special that God should single us out for immortality and not the rest of his creation? And for a while, I'm afraid to say, I lost my faith. It was not until I started to believe . . . Secretly believe . . . that the rest of God's creatures must have souls as well . . . that my faith began to return. And everything started to feel whole again.

OLIVER. And is that what you believe now?

KATHERINE. It's what I believed then. When I was young and innocent. But I'm a grown woman now. And I know how things go in the world.

OLIVER. Pretty as it sounds . . . there are many people in this country who would consider that an admission of heresy. And not so very long ago, young lady . . . they would have had you brought to the stake.

KATHERINE. Oh.

OLIVER. But not any more, I hasten to add. These days if someone's opinion is a little too . . . *unusual*, shall we say? What we do . . . we talk to them. That's all. For weeks on end if necessary. And then we lead them in the paths of righteousness.

JOHN. And if all else fails . . . ship them off to America. Isn't that right, Noll?

OLIVER. If all else fails. Yes.

KATHERINE. Let's start, shall we?

OLIVER. By all means.

KATHERINE. I've laid out a couple of places.

He gets up and then sits down in one of the places, JOHN *sitting in the other.*

You wouldn't want to pack me off to the Americas, would you?

JOHN. No, my dear. Of course he wouldn't. Heresy is one thing. *Innocence* is something else entirely. Wouldn't you agree, Noll?

OLIVER. Unreservedly so . . . John. And increasingly a rarity I fear. In this all-too-knowing age.

He spears a slice of ham with his knife and pushes it all into his mouth.

Did you bring a little salt?

KATHERINE. Sorry. But I don't think I did.

She searches in the hamper.

OLIVER. This ham is good. Very good. But I've always been partial to a little salt.

KATHERINE. I meant to bring some. But I don't think I packed it in the hamper.

OLIVER. Don't worry.

He cuts off a large piece of cheese and pushes that into his mouth. Mixing it up with the ham. And then swills it all down with a gulp of wine.

KATHERINE. Shall I cut you some cheese?

JOHN. Just a thin slice. Please.

OLIVER. I'm enjoying this. Good food. Good wine. The company of good friends. I'm at one with God and all his creation. What more could a man want in this life?

He puts a hand to his mouth. Trying to cover his need to belch.

Pardon me.

JOHN. And just think . . . this is nothing more than an inkling. The merest hint of all that is to come.

OLIVER. Amen to that.

KATHERINE *passes* JOHN *a piece of bread and a thin slice of cheese. He talks between mouthfuls.*

JOHN. If we hold fast and redouble our efforts . . . then through the sweat of our brow and the strength of our will . . . Jerusalem shall be built anew in this, God's chosen country.

OLIVER. 'And I saw the holy city, the new Jerusalem, coming down from God out of Heaven.'

JOHN. 'And I heard a great voice out of Heaven, saying. "Behold, the tabernacle of God is with men".'

OLIVER. 'And he will dwell with them, and they shall be his people.'

JOHN. Amen. Amen.

KATHERINE. 'And God shall wipe away all tears from their eyes; and there shall be no more death, neither sorrow nor crying . . . neither shall there be any more pain.'

Silence. This is the centre of the play. The eye of the storm.

OLIVER. Well said, my dear. Well said. It does my heart good
to listen to a young woman who knows her Bible. It's a sure
sign of the times. A clear manifestation of the *righteousness*
of our actions these past ten years. For is it not written in
the Book of Proverbs that 'A virtuous woman is a crown to
her husband, but she that maketh ashamed is as rottenness
in his bones'?

KATHERINE. Amen to that. Amen.

She cuts a slice of ham for herself.

But I can't help hoping that in this New Jerusalem . . . you
both talk about so earnestly . . . we women will be valued
for ourselves, not just as someone holding our husband's
hand, so to speak. For is it not Jeremiah who says that 'a
woman shall *compass* a man'?

Silence.

OLIVER. *Does* he say that?

JOHN. Yes. I think so.

OLIVER. Really?

JOHN. Yes, Noll. I think you'll find he does. Chapter 31.
Verse 22.

OLIVER. Mm.

They eat in silence for a while.

KATHERINE. Can I get you anything? A little more cheese,
perhaps?

OLIVER (*unbuttoning his jacket*). Not just at the moment,
thank you.

KATHERINE. John?

JOHN. Yes . . . Cut me a modest slice of ham, if you'd be so
kind.

She cuts the ham.

KATHERINE. My mother taught me to read. When I was very
little. And for a while, the Bible was the only book we kept

in the house. So despite my father's repeated warnings, I'd read it from cover to cover. Over and over again.

JOHN (*laughing*). What a very difficult little girl you must've been. I can just see you. Smiling like an angel when you wanted something. But hot-eyed and tear-stained when you couldn't get your way.

OLIVER. Damn these hot sweats. Past few months I've been getting them almost every day. Demeaning for a man of my age and standing, wouldn't you say?

KATHERINE. You eat too quickly. It isn't good for you.

She passes JOHN *a slice of ham.*

OLIVER. Leaves me prostrate for a few hours. And then . . . Glory be . . . it goes away again. It's not a serious condition . . . I don't think . . . but it does seem to wear me out. Drains me of all patience and energy. And these days I need all the energy *and* the patience I can muster.

JOHN. And what does your doctor prescribe for this condition?

OLIVER. A variety of foul-tasting concoctions, which he's been forcing down my throat of late. All of them with the most inscrutable Latin names. It's beyond me, I'm afraid, to single one out.

KATHERINE. Can I pour you a little more wine?

OLIVER. Wine? Oh yes. Certainly. Please.

KATHERINE. Hold your hand still.

She pours more wine into OLIVER*'s glass, and then into* JOHN*'s.*

JOHN. And what is he putting into these medicines? What substances does he use?

OLIVER. I don't know. I don't ask.

JOHN. You haven't ever considered the *possibility* . . . and it is no more than that, I hasten to add . . . that these medicines you're taking . . . far from alleviating the symptoms you're complaining of . . . might in actual fact be bringing them about?

OLIVER. What are you implying?

JOHN. A few years ago . . . desperate to find a cure for my
failing eyesight . . . I consulted a man who was by repute . . .
one of the best doctors in the world.

KATHERINE. John. Please.

JOHN. This was in Paris, you understand, where all the best
doctors supposedly are.

OLIVER. So they say.

JOHN. Once inside the surgery – instantly recognisable by the
charnel nature of its stench – I was forcibly sat in a chair
and then held down by a well-muscled assistant . . . while
the doctor himself . . . He was French. Naturally.

KATHERINE. Please don't.

JOHN. While the doctor himself first cauterised my brow with
a hot iron, then pricked the skin with a needle and drew a
thread through the resulting aperture. This was in order to
allow the noxious vapours to 'issue forth from the eye'.
Or so I was told.

*KATHERINE puts her fingers to her ears and hums quietly
to herself, trying to shut out his words.*

It was, as you can well imagine, a humiliating and
extraordinarily painful process, which was repeated many
times in the course of the treatments. Strangely conceived,
barbarously executed and entirely without effect. So ghastly
was the experience and so utterly futile, that I began to
wonder if the doctor had some other purpose in mind.

OLIVER. Purpose? What sort of a purpose?

JOHN. I mean, other than his professed objective of effecting
a cure. Something altogether darker. Born of a cold
curiosity. Something more akin to the aims of a torturer
perhaps. Or even a murderer.

OLIVER. I wouldn't go as far as to say that. Yes . . . they're
scoundrels by and large, I concede that. But the best of
them, in my experience, are both genius and charlatan in

more or less equal measure. And when you fancy death is
knocking at your door, you have to put your trust in
somebody. It's human nature, John.

Silence.

I had a dream the other night. A strange dream. I was sitting
in a wilderness of rocks and stones. No living thing in sight.
Shivering with cold. Then a man in rags came up to me.
And he gave me a coat. Heavy material. Rich embroidery.
'You keep it,' I said. 'Your need is by far the greater.' But he
wouldn't take no for an answer. So in the end . . . to please
him . . . I put it on.

He lies back, closing his eyes.

And it fitted so well, it might have been made for me.
A truly wondrous garment. But when I tried to take it off,
I found that the fabric had stuck to my skin. And the harder
I pulled, the more I tore my own flesh.

Silence.

What do you make of that, then?

JOHN. Extraordinary.

KATHERINE. Does anyone want any more of anything?
Before I put it all away.

She searches through the hamper.

Where are the pears? I'm sure I packed some pears. There's
a drop of wine left. If anyone wants to finish the bottle?

JOHN. Not for me. Thank you.

KATHERINE. Oliver?

No response.

Oliver? How about you?

JOHN. I think he's asleep.

Silence.

KATHERINE. Poor man.

JOHN *lies back in the grass.*

The burden of the world upon his shoulders.

JOHN. Come lie next to me, Katherine dearest. And we'll join him in a little nap. It won't do us any harm. That elderberry wine was awfully strong.

She pours the last of the wine into her own glass and gulps it down.

KATHERINE. Not just at the moment.

JOHN. Why not, for goodness' sake?

KATHERINE. I don't feel like it. Besides . . . when you treat me like a piece of your property, John, not unnaturally, I have a tendency to recoil.

JOHN. Oh don't start all that.

KATHERINE. You're such a bully sometimes. Telling that awful story about your eyes. You know how much I hate it. Why do you have to get your own way all the time? What about *my* feelings? Don't they count for anything?

JOHN. Of course they do. Come over here and let me make it up to you.

KATHERINE. No.

Silence.

Not unless you say you're sorry. And you promise not to do it again.

JOHN. I promise. And I'm sorry. Really sorry.

She sits by him.

KATHERINE. You'd better mean it.

JOHN. Oh I do.

They embrace and lie back in the grass. Folded in each other's arms.

End of Act One.

ACT TWO

OLIVER *is still asleep, lying on his back.* JOHN *and* KATHERINE *are sleeping too, entwined in each other's arms. The flute can be heard. An ancient tune from our primitive past.*

GEORGE *enters. He stares down at the sleeping faces. Stooping low over* OLIVER, *baring his teeth. There's a pagan feel to the image. A scene from Greek mythology.*

KATHERINE *wakes. She and* GEORGE *stare at one another for a long time. Eventually she rubs her eyes, breaking the spell.*

KATHERINE. John. John.

She shakes him by the shoulder.

John!

GEORGE *bounds away into the undergrowth.*

JOHN. What? What is it?

KATHERINE. I am awake, aren't I?

JOHN. Awake? Of course you are. And so am I. Don't be silly. Just think about it for a moment. If we're neither of us awake . . . am I, in this moment, dreaming about you? Or are you dreaming about me?

KATHERINE. *What*? Oh, John. I don't know. It's just that it was all so strange.

JOHN. We can't very well both be dreaming the same thing at the same time . . . that would be very very unlikely. But not impossible actually.

KATHERINE. John. Stop it. You're making me even more confused.

JOHN. Well, you did ask.

KATHERINE. It was such a strange feeling. As I opened my
eyes just now. Just for an instant. It was as if the world of
the ancients had suddenly come to life. A world of sylvans
and dryads. Echo and Narcissus. Pan playing on his pipe.

She shivers.

But now I think about it . . . it was probably that horrible
old man stealing from our hamper.

JOHN. Nonsense. He wouldn't dare.

He holds her in his arms.

I enjoyed our little sleep just now. Lying in the grass,
sprawled like Adam in that earliest garden. The weight of
your head in the crook of my arm – even if it did give me
pins and needles after a while – the softness of your touch.
A most congenial foretaste . . . I thought . . . of our future
life together.

KATHERINE. It wasn't a sinful thing to do, was it?

JOHN. No. Of course not.

KATHERINE. There was so much pleasure in it . . . I fear it
must be wrong.

JOHN. How can anything so innocent and so utterly agreeable
be wrong?

KATHERINE. Our God is a just God. And a good God. But
he's also a God of wrath, is he not?

OLIVER *almost wakes with a stertorous choking sound.*

Or so I've read in the Old Testament.

JOHN. That was in ages past, my darling. In the New
Jerusalem . . . I promise you . . . everything will be right
and in its proper place.

KATHERINE. So you keep saying.

OLIVER *moans in his sleep.*

Perhaps we should go in now. Nature is beautiful. But it's
possibly better appreciated from the safety of your own
fireside.

She wraps up the ham and packs it away.

JOHN. I'll wash the plates, shall I?

KATHERINE. There's no need really. They're not very dirty.

JOHN. I think I'd better do it. The idea of packing away soiled crockery makes me rather edgy.

He starts to collect the plates and the beakers.

KATHERINE. He's ill, isn't he? More than he lets on.

JOHN. Yes. I believe he is.

KATHERINE. Poor thing.

She wraps up the cheese and puts it away.

We didn't eat much of the cheese.

JOHN. No . . . Where's your plate?

JOHN is now close to KATHERINE, on his hands and knees. His hand tentatively searching the grass in front of her.

KATHERINE. I don't – Oh. I'm kneeling on it.

He adds the plate to the two he's already carrying.

JOHN. As you know, my opinion of the medical profession is hardly uncritical, but that personal physician of his . . . Bates, or whatever he calls himself . . . does seem particularly suspect. The man's an avowed Royalist.

KATHERINE. But he is treating him properly, isn't he? To the best of his ability.

JOHN. One would hope so, yes. Insofar as that's actually possible with men of his calling.

JOHN sets off towards the stream.

KATHERINE. John.

JOHN. What?

KATHERINE. Perhaps we'd better wake him up. It doesn't do to fall too deeply asleep in the heat of the day. What do you think?

JOHN. Wake him. Yes.

KATHERINE. Can't *you* do it? I don't know him very well. Makes me feel a bit presumptuous.

JOHN. Oh. For goodness' sake, he's not going to bite you.

And he disappears from view. Silence. Then KATHERINE *sits down next to* OLIVER. *She shakes him gently by the shoulder.*

KATHERINE. Mr Cromwell. I think it's time you woke up.

OLIVER *opens his eyes.*

OLIVER. Where am I?

She laughs.

KATHERINE. We're in the grounds of Hampton Court. Somewhere in the park. I don't know where exactly.

He stares at her.

I'm Katherine Woodstock. I came here with John Milton.

OLIVER. Of course. Yes.

He stands up.

Sorry. I didn't recognise you for a moment. Couldn't think what I was doing out here in the open air . . . in the company of a young lady. Disconcerting, really.

He remembers to secure his breeches, which he had loosened before he fell asleep.

Always enjoyed female company, I have to say. Never seem to've got enough of it. What with one thing and another. Especially a women with a head on her shoulders. You ever met Johnnie Lambert's wife, Frances?

KATHERINE *shakes her head,*

A very handsome woman. Talks a lot of sense. Always enjoy her company. Very stimulating. I know people say things behind our back. In a slanderous and most ungenerous fashion. But God alone knows the truth.

Awkward silence.

My wife is a very caring woman and I love her dearly, but she's not blessed with an over-abundance of mental energy. And now if you'll excuse me, I really must answer the call of nature.

He sets off into the undergrowth. Silence. KATHERINE *is sitting on her own now. The flute sounds distantly.* JOHN's *voice drifts in on the breeze, declaiming his own verse.*

JOHN.
Adam, the goodliest man of men since born
His sons; the fairest of her daughters Eve.
Under a tuft of shade that on a green
Stood whispering soft, by a fresh fountain side,
They sat them down . . .

OLIVER (*off*). What was that? I didn't quite catch that!

KATHERINE. It's John!

OLIVER (*off*). What?

KATHERINE. He's speaking in verse!

OLIVER (*off*). He's what?

KATHERINE. Verse! He's talking in verse!

OLIVER (*off*). *Verse?*

KATHERINE. Yes!

OLIVER (*off*). I've been keeping him pretty busy these past few years. I'm surprised he's got any time for it!

OLIVER *returns, tucking his shirt into his breeches. An awkward silence follows.*

JOHN.
Nectarine fruits, which the compliant boughs
Yielded them, sidelong as they sat recline
On the soft downy bank damasked with flowers
The savoury pulp they chew, and in the rind
Still as they thirsted, scoop the brimming stream.

Silence.

KATHERINE. He often declaims his poetry like that. He says it helps him to remember it. Now he can't jot things down any more.

OLIVER. I see.

KATHERINE. He's supposed to be washing the plates. By the 'brimming stream'. But he's probably forgotten why he ever went down there.

OLIVER. Perhaps one of us should go down and remind him.

KATHERINE. Noll . . . I can call you Noll, can't I?

OLIVER. Of course.

KATHERINE. I mean, I can't very well call you Mr Cromwell all the time. And Oliver sounds too formal somehow.

OLIVER. Call me Noll. All my friends call me Noll.

KATHERINE. Well . . . Noll. There's something I'd like to ask you.

OLIVER. Fire away.

KATHERINE. John's always talking about the New Jerusalem. It's something he's always hoping is going to happen very soon.

OLIVER. Yes?

KATHERINE. Well. As far as I can see, the likelihood of it just seems to get further away.

OLIVER. I know. I know. It's like trying to grasp a bubble. The harder you try, the more likely you are to burst it.

KATHERINE. And I can always tell when it's praying on his mind because he gets so bad tempered.

OLIVER. Yes. I know about that, too.

KATHERINE. So is this a belief you share with him? A perfect world, growing out of the very imperfect one we've already got?

Silence.

And assuming that you do . . . What's it going to be like?
I mean . . . What's life actually going to be like, here in
England, when it finally happens?

OLIVER. You've gone straight to the heart of it, young lady.
It's a question that's confounded better minds than mine.
Aye. And your husband's, too.

KATHERINE. He's not my husband yet. Quite.

OLIVER. All I can tell you . . . at this time . . . Paradise . . .
the New Jerusalem . . . call it what you like . . . it's a state
of being with God. The whole of our society at one with
God. And if that sounds a bit vague, I'm sorry. Every night I
beseech the Lord to make his purpose clear to me. In the
anguish of prayer. But revelations do not follow with the
dawn, I'm afraid to say. As they once did.

JOHN *returns unnoticed with the washed plates and
beakers.*

At Naseby, for example . . . at that critical moment in the
battle, when things can go either way. Just when the enemy
must've surely felt that they were getting the upper hand,
I suddenly experienced . . . and quite unlooked for, I have
to say . . . what I can only call a surge of innermost joy.
A certainty that my purposes and God's purposes were one
and the same. Extraordinary. Like riding a wave. And this
feeling was so intense. So utterly exhilarating . . . I was
quite unable to contain my laughter. Yes . . . laughter. It
simply burst out of me. At the height of battle. As men died
in agony around me.

KATHERINE. How very strange.

OLIVER. Yes. Indeed. But in the years that've gone by . . .
any sense I had of absolute righteousness has faded. God's
purposes have not unrolled before me as they once
promised to do. His Kingdom still seems as far away as it
ever was. And I'm tormented by the thought that if God
wasn't with me on that day, then why was my heart so filled
with joy?

KATHERINE. I don't know. I really couldn't say.

OLIVER. We're all susceptible to Satan's influence, my dear. There's none of us exempt.

KATHERINE. I know.

OLIVER. But after long and agonised nights, seeking the voice of Christ in my heart . . . I have come to the conclusion that the inspiration I was filled with . . . on that day . . . coming as it surely did from God . . . was a substance too perfect . . . too pure and undiluted for the cracked and imperfect vessel that has tried . . . is still *trying* . . . to contain it.

Silence.

I'm sorry, I'm not making myself very clear. Perhaps if I'd been stronger. And purer in heart. It may all have worked out for the better.

JOHN. Oh come now, Oliver. Forgive me if I'm speaking out of turn. What you seem to be saying is that the fate of the whole country is somehow lodged inside you. And bound up with your fate. Subject to your moods and digestion, as a good meal might be, say. Which . . . if you don't mind me saying so . . . is taking one's sense of responsibility a little far.

He moves uncertainly towards the other two, a protective arm held out in front of him.

I mean, because you hoped . . . *believed* rather . . . that events were going to work out in a certain way, it isn't your fault necessarily if it hasn't happened like that. You're not the be-all. And the end-all. No matter how often lesser mortals might tell you that you are. Katherine. Where are you?

KATHERINE. I'm here.

She runs to him. Takes his hand.

JOHN. Thank you, my dearest. Am I back where I was?

KATHERINE. No. Not quite. There's a little way to go.

She leads him towards OLIVER. Resolutely standing his ground.

JOHN. You see . . . For the New Jerusalem to happen, we must – *all* of us – want it to happen. It's not going to be handed down to us out of the clouds. In a miraculous apparition. The Almighty rending the firmament and showering us with gifts of corn, wine and oil and all the rest of it. Such beliefs belong to our primitive past. We're living in the modern age. The New Jerusalem will have to be built. Physically and materially. *Built*! Out of our dreams and our ideas. From the plans we draw up. From the strength of our hands. The sweat of our brow. And our absolute commitment to see the thing through.

He holds out the plates.

KATHERINE. I'll put those in the hamper.

She takes the plates and the beakers and then kneels down, packing them in the hamper.

OLIVER. You sound very sure of yourself.

JOHN. Yes. Well . . . I am.

OLIVER. There's no room in your heart for doubt?

JOHN. No. Not the way I feel at the moment. The future doesn't seem to be in any doubt at all. The New Jerusalem is very close. It's not a question of 'if it's going to happen' . . . in my view. It's only a question of 'when'.

KATHERINE. Will it be in our lifetime, John?

JOHN. I would dearly hope so. But it's possible that all we're doing is preparing the way for the next generation. Or the generation after that. Or even generations yet to come. And in a sense, it doesn't matter. Why worry about the nature of our physical involvement when what we're building is our spiritual inheritance?

OLIVER. I still don't see how you can be so sure.

JOHN. It's just that . . . there's an *inevitability* about it. We're not moving *towards* barbarism. Not as far as I can see. We're moving *away* from all that. And have been since the fall of Greece and Rome. Inexorably so. The great river of history is sweeping us towards the fertile plains of civilisation, co-operation and harmony. Not the other way around. I mean, you can't argue that history is flowing in the other bloody direction, can you?

OLIVER *remains silent.*

In all honesty . . . No matter how desperate the times we live in seem to be.

OLIVER. It's a point I'm not contesting, actually. I'm merely interested to know the grounds for your overwhelming sense of confidence . . . in an area where I for one tend to experience a fair amount of doubt and uncertainty. That's all.

JOHN. Of course. Yes. The point I was leading to, however –

OLIVER. And I'm not enamoured of your language, by the by.

JOHN. Sorry. I was carried away. Sheer exuberance, I'm afraid. No blasphemy intended.

OLIVER. We're not brawling in a tavern.

JOHN. No . . .

OLIVER. We're trying to tease out the truth. From the knotted mass of lies and half-truths that inevitably confront us, whenever we put our minds to matters of this kind.

JOHN. Yes. Exactly.

OLIVER. But you're right about one thing: these are desperate times.

Silence.

JOHN. Indeed.

Silence.

What I was going on to say . . . however . . . having pretty much shown I think that history is with us in this matter . . .

OLIVER. Yes. I think we can agree . . . that's a point you've quite definitely made.

JOHN. And before my unfortunate lapse into the vernacular . . . for which I humbly beg forgiveness . . .

OLIVER. You're forgiven. Now could you –

JOHN. I can't think what came over me.

OLIVER. No.

JOHN. I mean, I'm not –

OLIVER. No. Could you please come to the –

JOHN. It's not something I'm prone to. In the normal course of events.

OLIVER. I'm sure. Now get on with it.

JOHN. Yes.

Silence.

What I *intended* to say . . . before you so rightly interrupted me . . . was that in order to take the next step in our journey towards the New Jerusalem, we must try and define the nature, the *structure* of the society we're going to build. Define our goal, so to speak, so that we might all the more clearly see the most effective way of getting there.

OLIVER. Go on.

JOHN. The vision I have is of a nation of free men . . . yes, and women too . . . free to worship God in whatsoever way they choose. Living in comfort, working in moderation. Never going hungry. A democratic nation, run by its citizens for the benefit of its citizens. Where everyone has an equal right to property. Wealth. Education. Opportunity.

KATHERINE. Amen.

JOHN. And all the other blessings of a truly representative society. In my mind's eye . . . and almost, I suppose, with the intensity of a child . . . I see a citadel high on a mountain. Sun-splashed, with pinnacles of stone soaring up to Heaven through the clouds. Like the hopes of men reaching up to God. And below, the ever-open gateway. I see multitudes of people drawn towards it. The poor. The downtrodden. The dispossessed. Walking up the mountain hand in hand. Shouting. Singing hymns. Paeans of joy. Longing for justice. Peace. Learning. And the gratification of desire.

OLIVER. Yes. That's all very well. But what you're actually taking about is a republic, isn't it? Come on. Own up. A republic. On the Roman model.

JOHN. Well, Roman-ish . . . yes. But only very loosely . . .

OLIVER. I thought as much.

JOHN. I mean, I wouldn't want to appropriate any of their notions of Empire, for example. Their religion. Their appetite for servitude. Or the the cruelty and banality of their pastimes.

OLIVER. No. Of course not.

JOHN. But the ideal remains. Shining and golden. Beckoning us into the future. Just think of it for a moment. A republic, in which matters of state would be decided, not by a single individual with an inherited right . . . nor by the ramshackle chaos of an elected Parliament . . . but by a senate of the most responsible, the most able, the most enlightened men in society.

OLIVER. An elite, you mean?

JOHN. Not as such. No. Simply the best minds available. And rather than clutter this main assembly with all the problems of provincial government, from which . . . I mean, even in geographical terms it would always be somewhat remote . . . a network of local senates would be established, each modelled on the main assembly and set up to deal with the specific needs of a particular area of the country.

OLIVER. I see. And how would the people you envisage sitting in these assemblies be selected? Not through an inherited right, surely?

JOHN. No.

OLIVER. And if by appointment . . . of course . . . who would do the appointing?

JOHN. Exactly.

OLIVER. It must be by election, then?

JOHN. Not that either.

OLIVER. No?

JOHN. No. Men and women of virtue and intelligence would virtually select themselves. Taking the reins of government . . . as of right! And serving the state for as long as they felt able to do so. At which point, naturally, they would step down, in favour of the most accomplished of the next generation. And so it would go on.

OLIVER. Mmm. And if they wouldn't go?

JOHN. They would be persuaded to go.

OLIVER. And if they still wouldn't go?

JOHN. Then one would have to persist until they finally agreed.

OLIVER *laughs.*

OLIVER. That's not as easy as it might sound. I've spent the best part of thirty years trying to persuade people in Parliament to all sorts of things. And believe me, I've never once known them to agree about anything.

He stops laughing.

That's been the problem, really. From the very beginning.

He circles round, getting his thoughts in order.

Mr Milton . . . in this idealised world you're proposing so enthusiastically, you make little mention of God. He does have a place, I take it, in this republic of yours?

Silence.

JOHN. I'll answer your question with a question of my own, if it's all the same to you.

OLIVER. Very well.

JOHN. In all your outpourings on the subject, My Lord General, I only hear you talk about '*God's* will', never your own. Nothing at all about your *own* desires. Does that make you a man without personal ambition?

Silence.

God dwells in the hearts of men. And it is through the excellence of our achievements that his purposes will be revealed.

OLIVER *is coldly angry. He doesn't show much of it on the surface. He sniffs. Gathering his resources to try and break* JOHN*'s position.*

OLIVER. And that's how you see God, is it . . . revealing his divinity through the minds and the hearts of men?

JOHN. Yes it is. More or less.

OLIVER. And nothing is going to shake you from this belief, I would assume. It's set in stone.

JOHN. My vision is unshakeable.

OLIVER. The problem is, of course, that most of the people I meet these days have an unshakeable belief in something or other. All them damned sectaries we've been talking about. Ranters. Fifth Monarchists and the like. And all of them holding their particular belief to be the only truth in the universe. Arguing back with Pentecostal heat and tongues of fire in a regular pandemonium of din and blather. I'll tell you something. If I believed people in proportion to the intensity of their faith and their principles, I'd be giving credence to some of the most dangerous lunatics in the country. Certainty of belief, Mr Milton . . . is no substitute for truth.

JOHN. I wasn't . . . for a moment . . . suggesting that it was.

OLIVER. Good. Good. Well, that's something to be thankful for. So let me just ask you something. How are you going to turn this vision of yours into *reality*? Mmm? Write *more* pamphlets? Lie in wait for sympathetic Members of Parliament outside Westminster Hall and chivvy them into drawing up a suitable bill? A bill that would see them all out of a job, incidentally. Or what? Turn the world on its head again and put us all through another bloody revolution? Sacrifice this generation for the future of the next? Because, let's face it, that's what it would probably involve.

JOHN. No. Not necessarily.

OLIVER. 'Not necessarily.' I see. So let's just get one thing straight, shall we? One little thing . . .

He wipes his brow with his shirt tails.

Just how far are you prepared to go, then? You *personally*. In order to bring this republic of yours into being?

Silence.

JOHN. I'll do whatever has to be done.

OLIVER. And if this . . . of necessity . . . involves going the whole hog . . . as they say . . . could you endure all the suffering and the killing that would undoubtedly ensue?

JOHN. I don't see it would necessarily come to that.

OLIVER. But what if it did . . . come to that? What if bloodshed and terror were the only way?

JOHN *remains silent.*

I see where you're going, Mr Milton. And I'm not sure that I like it. I mean, visions are all very well . . . as long as they remain just that . . . *visions*. No. Listen. Because I'm telling you . . . once the dreamer gets off his backside and starts to try and give substance to his visions in *reality*, that's when the trouble starts.

KATHERINE. Why trouble necessarily?

OLIVER. Because the dreamer by definition's got no grounding in the give-and-take, the hurly-burly of political debate and the grind of administration . . . believing as he does that certainty is proof of righteousness . . . he thinks that all he needs to do . . . *all* he needs to do is define his ideas strongly enough and make his point, you know, with clarity and purpose, and everyone will just simply fall into line. He doesn't compromise, or rethink his position in any way, he just insists. And goes on insisting. Until finally, instead of arguing with his opponents, he's brushing them aside. Wishing to hell he could dispose of them altogether. Changing by degrees from a hapless idealist, who wouldn't hurt the proverbial fly, to a stubborn fanatic, bending the people to his absolute will, whether they wish it or no. It's a horrible transmogrification. The beginnings of which you might just possibly start to recognise.

JOHN. No. No. Now listen.

OLIVER. The point is –

JOHN. No. I've had the same thoughts, Noll. The same fears . . . the very same . . . And after searching my heart . . . I can honestly say . . .

OLIVER. The – the –

JOHN. That I'm free of any such delu –

OLIVER. The point *is* . . . Mr Milton. Before you can start telling people what to do, you have to experience the reality of power. What can be done. And what can't be done. What you can make happen . . . with a bit of guile and patience. And what's best left alone. Otherwise . . . *otherwise* . . . a man becomes so fixed in his intentions, he don't care no more about the consequences. He'll do anything. Anything at all to get his beliefs across. People can suffer. Die in agony. *Starve*. It doesn't matter. So long as he's closer to his goal, which need I remind you is the foundation of God's Kingdom here on earth. And so with the deepest irony imaginable, he might think he's building paradise. But he's not. He's the serpent in the garden . . . bringing Hell with him instead.

Silence.

You picture a city in the sunshine . . . under a blue sky. A thriving city. Beautifully proportioned. Prosperous. Just. Full of virtuous and cultured people. I picture one in ruin. Devastated by years of war and civil strife. Plague and famine. Worse than what we've been through. Much worse. Prisoners lashed to the cannon's mouth. Dismembered bodies jammed onto iron railings. Teachers hanging from their doorposts. Dead children in the playing fields. Unburied corpses in the street. I tell you . . . if that's what we have to go through to reach perfection, Mr Milton . . .

then maybe perfection just ain't worth striving for. So let's just do but what we can. Eh? And wait for God to make his move. Let's not try and force his hand.

JOHN. I'm not. I'm not doing that. Don't . . . don't dare think me so presumptuous, My Lord General.

He moves around with increasing agitation, careless of the limits imposed by his blindness.

And anyway, it seems to me that God has made his intentions perfectly clear already. To all of us. All God's Englishmen. I mean, we've all of us experienced it. That moment of absolute certainty. Just as you did at Naseby. At the height of battle. With laughter in your heart.

He walks awkwardly into a tree.

KATHERINE. John . . . !

JOHN. I'm all right. I'm all right. Don't worry.

He holds a hand over his eye. Dabs at it with his neckerchief.

So let us *unite* in this knowledge. All those of us who know. And know equally. In the eternal spirit of our being. And let us look forward in confidence. To the coming of the New Jerusalem. Whenever that may be. And do all that we can . . . to level the ground as it were. And to smooth the way.

KATHERINE. You've hurt your eye.

JOHN. It's nothing.

KATHERINE. Let me look.

She takes his neckerchief and screws up one of the corners. Preparing to dab away any intruding dirt.

Poor vulnerable eyes. That seem to see everything and yet see nothing at all.

JOHN. Don't fuss.

KATHERINE. Perhaps we should go indoors now.

JOHN. No. No. No.

KATHERINE. Too much exposure to nature, it would seem,

affects one's sense of what is proper.

JOHN. Lord General. You seem to think I'm fanatical for believing as I do. I'm not. I'm hopeful, that's all. Just because I haven't been refined, as it were, in the crucible of politics . . . doesn't mean that my ideas aren't golden necessarily. That they are, by definition, dross and without true worth.

KATHERINE. Hold still.

She flicks a speck of dirt out of the corner of his eye.

JOHN. On the contrary . . . it's good, I'd say . . . that I haven't had to compromise my convictions and trade them in the common marketplace. More than that . . . It's *vital* . . . that *someone* at least is speaking out for what they know to be true. And not padding about in this political half-world of yours, where conviction is emasculated and compromise extolled. Compromise isn't a *virtue*, you know, it's the unfortunate result of people not being able to agree. And nothing more.

KATHERINE. Finished now.

She puts the neckerchief back into his hand.

JOHN. Might it not be, Lord General, that all these years of accommodation and adjustment are finally taking their toll? That you've trimmed your sail to such an extent that you aren't actually going anywhere any more? Age does that to people. Tires them out. Drains away their energy. Blunts what little enthusiasm they have left. 'Anything for a quiet life.' That's what they say, isn't it? Well, I'll be fifty in a couple of years . . . Well on the way, some would say, to wooden teeth, milk sops and a nightcap. But at least I know I'm alive. And if I know I'm alive it's because I dare to dream. Not for a watered-down version of whatever it is you're going to arrive at after you and your Parliamentary colleagues've squeezed all the life out of it, but for a true vision, whole and undiminished, distilling all my convictions in the imminent coming of the Lord and the ultimate perfectibility of man.

OLIVER *gathers himself for one final assault.*

OLIVER. You're impossible. You know that? Self-opinionated. Vainglorious. And stubborn as a mule. When your mind's made up about something, it's set in stone for ever, it would seem. Like the tablets of Moses come down from the mountain. I could show you a pig. And I'd say: 'Look here. Smell the thing. Feel its snout. And its ears. The ring in its nose. And see there at t' other end. The tail and its terrible arse.' And if you'd previously set your mind to it, you'd still swear blind it were a horse! And I'm not saying that because you've lost your sight. Mr Milton. The darkening of your vision is a pity to us all. No. It's the darkness inside that worries me. The fact that you're so full of your own righteousness, God help you, you're blind to any opinion other than your own.

He strides around. Fighting to control his rage.

Here I am . . . for pity's sake . . . trying to give you some idea . . . of the simple realities . . . the *practicalities* of power . . . of what happens when you take the reins into your own hands . . . and suddenly find yourself responsible for the lives and the destinies of millions . . . Yes, *millions* of people. It's a very sobering responsibility.

JOHN. I don't doubt it –

OLIVER. I mean, I'd expect you to listen with a little humility, sir. And not come farting back at me, like some preposterous angel in a cloud . . . with all this – what should I call it? – this arrogant flimmer-flammer of personal conviction and revelation . . . this *insubstantial* . . . metaphysical speculation . . . against which – with people of your bent and inclination – there's never any gainsay!

He pauses for breath. Red in the face. Hardly articulate.

You can't go nowhere without there's the will of the people behind you. Nowhere at all. You can't force them to believe as you believe. Bully them. Chivvy them. Terrorise them into a change of heart. It just isn't possible. Because to force your beliefs onto people against their will is to drag them to the very pit of Hell. Always assuming, of course . . .

they haven't turned on you by then, cut out your tripes and stuck your head up on a pole. No. Before anything truly radical is possible in this quarrelsome, most disputatious country of ours, you've got to come to a proper agreement of the people. All of them. And that, believe me, is a labour so arduous, so utterly unfathomable, it would have defeated the mighty Hercules himself.

His breathing steadies.

Listen. Just four years ago, when I summoned that last Parliament, the 'Barebones Parliament' people call it . . . I hand-picked the most 'responsible', the most 'able', the most 'enlightened' men I could find to serve on it. Qualities you were yourself recommending but a short while ago. Surely these men were the saints come again, I thought, leading us into the Promised Land. I honestly felt we were standing on the threshold of the Eternal Kingdom. And what happened? They couldn't *agree*! Not about policy. Principle. Protocol. Not about anything! Not even about the time of day. Or when they might possibly adjourn for dinner. It was a most bitterly dispiriting and salutary experience. Everyone convinced of the uncompromised virginity of their own beliefs. Nothing but rancour and argument. Squalor and pandemonium. The Tower of Babel come again.

He rummages in the hamper and tugs out the wine bottle.

I tell you, the only reason I accepted the Protectorship was to deliver the country from this ministry of fools.

He pulls out the cork.

KATHERINE. Just a moment. I'll get you something to drink from.

She searches in the hamper for a beaker.

I only packed it all away because I thought we were going. I wasn't trying to say you shouldn't have another. Or anything like that.

KATHERINE *takes the wine bottle and pours out the last of the wine into the beaker.*

OLIVER. Of course, people've tried to say that my head's
been turned by all the pomp and circumstance, but don't you
listen to them. All I'm trying to do is see the country
through the next few years . . . Solvent, healthy and
undiminished in the world.

KATHERINE *hands him the wine.*

Thank you, my dear. Very civil of you.

*He sits down on the ground. Mops his brow with his shirt
front. He looks tired and drained.*

If you asked me what I was doing, I'd tell you I was
'getting by'. That's all.

He sips the wine.

You see, I've learned . . . that whatever you might want –
deep in the heart and in the very bowels of you – for the
furtherance of God's purposes and for the public good . . .
you've got to be prepared to put it all to one side, however
painful it might be to do so, if it's not commensurate with
the needs of the people you serve. See. Without their will
behind you, you're not going to achieve anything. Anything
lasting, that is. Write all the pamphlets you like. But unless
you can convince these people of your absolute *rightness*,
my son, then these visionary dreams of yours just ain't
worth twopence, I'm afraid.

JOHN *sulks on.*

Nothing to say for yourself?

JOHN. I don't enjoy being spoken to like that. May I remind
you that I'm not a child . . . to be reprimanded at the
parent's merest whim.

OLIVER. No. Sorry. I lost my temper. I went too far. It's a sin
to have a filthy temper like mine and to give it full rein. But
pride is a sin too, Mr Milton. Need I remind you that a true
penitent would have embraced such a castigation with open
arms.

JOHN. Would he now?

Silence.

A proud man . . . I probably . . . well, almost certainly am. And all the other unpleasant things I'm sure people say about me behind my back. But need I remind *you*, My Lord General, that a frank admission to the sin of pride, whilst it does little credit to a man's character, doesn't necessarily discredit the quality of his argument.

OLIVER *smiles.*

You see . . . despite all these grand words . . . and with the very best intentions I have no doubt . . . all you're doing really is letting things slide. I mean, you've more or less admitted as much yourself.

OLIVER. Oh. Is that all I'm doing? Well, thank you for reminding me. Thank you very much.

JOHN. So that what's actually happening . . . without anyone seemingly being aware of it . . . is that we're in real danger of sliding back into the state we were in when we started out, ten or so years ago.

OLIVER. Nonsense.

JOHN. No. It's true. You see . . . we *are*! Because no one's sure of their position any more. In the shifting ground of our 'new' society, people are running about like headless chickens, waiting for the King to come back and nail them to their rightful place. Ordinary people. In whom the idea of monarchy has become so ingrained that all their notions of government have become inextricably bound up with this idea of having someone in authority, with an inherited right, telling them all exactly what to do. Either a king like Charles Stuart. Or someone very like a king.

Silence.

Someone willing to bear the title and shoulder the responsibility of absolute rule.

OLIVER. Oh, come on. Don't be so coy, man. Out with it. Someone like me. That's what you're driving at, isn't it?

JOHN. Well, you have been offered the position.

OLIVER. Yes. And I turned it down.

JOHN. But only after a considerable period of deliberation.

OLIVER. There was a great deal to consider.

JOHN. Oh, was there? Was there really ?

KATHERINE. John. John.

JOHN. I mean, what kind of things were you *having* to consider? Because I thought we'd got rid of the whole idea of monarchy. I thought that was why we cut off the King's head. Not out of any sense of vindictiveness, but to put an end to that unfair, undemocratic, utterly outdated and altogether anomalous way of running the country. Not reinvent it in some bastardised form, simply because most people have been so conditioned over the centuries that they can't conceive of being governed in any other way.

OLIVER. They have to be governed *somehow*. We can't just sit back and let everything drift into chaos. There has to be a guiding hand. Changes have to be made.

JOHN. Yes, but not by going back to the very thing we were trying to get rid of in the first place.

OLIVER. Hang on a minute. Hang on. When we started out, it was never my intention to turn the system on its head. Never something I set out to do. But unfortunately . . . as the conflict progressed it became . . . more or less . . . an inevitability. So let's put things in their proper perspective here. Let's not get carried away. The killing of the King . . . was a *consequence* of our actions, not the objective that we all had in mind when we started out.

Silence.

I'll tell you something, though . . . If it wasn't for the stigma of kingship . . . the tainted history . . . of that most bloody institution . . . I'd crown myself tomorrow. Because I *know* the country would breathe a sigh of relief and then get down to the serious business of building towards prosperity.

He mops his face once more with his shirt front.

JOHN. So there *is* something about the idea of sovereignty that appeals to you, then?

OLIVER. Yes. But as I say . . . only in a *practical* sense. Only insofar as it might help me to get the job done.

JOHN. And so you're not at all tempted by the – what shall I say? – by the *trappings* of regality?

OLIVER. No.

JOHN. The sheer luxury of your present life. The food. The palaces you live in. People falling over themselves to get your attention. The fussing of innumerable guards and servants. And so on.

OLIVER. No!

KATHERINE. John. Please.

JOHN. I mean . . . who could blame you if this . . . *thing* has gone to your head?

KATHERINE. John. I really don't think you should –

JOHN. You're king in all but name already. It must seem like a very small step to take.

OLIVER. Mr Milton. What are you trying to say exactly?

JOHN. Don't allow your feelings for humanity to cloud your better judgement. I think that's all I'm trying to . . . One step further is a step into the abyss. For pity's sake, turn away from it. For is it not written in the Book of Proverbs: 'Therefore shall his calamity come suddenly.' And 'suddenly shall he be broken without remedy'?

Silence. KATHERINE *starts to cry*

Just think . . . The lives of our comrades . . . Sacrificed for nothing. Everything we've gained . . . thrown away as if it were a hand at cards.

OLIVER. You go too far, Mr Milton. You're like a hound with a fox. Get your teeth into something and you won't ever let it go. Were I not confident you were speaking from the heart, I'd've found your message quite intolerable. And

taken whatever measures were necessary to shut you up.
But this is not a matter between you and me, Mr Milton.
This is a matter between me and my God. A covenant
which, as you well know . . . has sustained me in the hours
of greatest darkness. And given me hope for the future.

He notices KATHERINE, *who is weeping quietly.*

For as it says in Isaiah: 'The earth shall be full of the
knowledge of the Lord, as the waters cover the sea.' And
I think that concludes the matter. My dear . . . why are you
crying?

KATHERINE (*through her tears*). I just wish you'd stop it.
That's all. Just stop it. This constant argument . . . I can't
stand it. I mean, where's it getting us? It seems so futile . . .

JOHN. Katy, it's all right. Don't upset yourself. What are mere
words when tears can be so eloquent?

KATHERINE. Don't patronise me.

JOHN. I'm not.

KATHERINE. Yes you are.

JOHN. No, Kate. I mean it. A tear is an intellectual thing. Isn't
that so, Oliver?

KATHERINE. Don't be so ridiculous.

JOHN *puts an arm round her.*

(*Shaking herself free.*) And please don't try and . . . *enclose*
me . . . like that. I am who I am. I'm not a part of you. At
least, not yet I'm not.

JOHN *coldly withdraws his arm.*

And as for having an idea in my head . . . that people might
find useful, stimulating . . . or even interesting . . . well,
that's an impossibility really, isn't it? Coming from
someone like me. It's as if I'm not really here.

OLIVER. Kate.

KATHERINE. A few years ago . . . when this Commonwealth
of ours was still in its early days. And everyone was talking

about the 'New Jerusalem' as if it was just around the corner. Just for a moment – and only for a moment, mind you – it was as if a curtain was suddenly pulled aside. And I . . . Well, people like me . . . *women* like me . . . got a glimpse of a different kind of life. I mean . . . different to the life my poor mother had, for example . . . As free as any man's.

A distant 'crack!' A broken branch – or a pistol shot. And then a flapping of wings as a flock of birds rises in the air.

The vision didn't last, of course. It wasn't long before the curtain was pulled tight shut once more. Almost before we'd had the chance to see what was *really* there. And since then, everything's muddled on . . . pretty much as it did before. All of us quietly getting on with our lives. Dutifully bringing up the next generation.

A cry of pain from some distance away.

JOHN. What was that?

OLIVER. I don't know. A bird maybe. An animal in a trap?

KATHERINE. Nothing's going to change in my lifetime, John. I don't care what you say. There's always going to be mothers weeping over their dead sons. And you know why? It's because you can't . . . men like you can't, anyway . . . can't just accept what you are . . . and what someone else is . . . and let things be.

Another cry.

You can't make allowances for the fact that other people believe something different and let it go at that. You have to go tearing at each other's throats. (*Weeping.*) Nothing's *ever* going to change. Not as far as I can see. There's always going to be wars. Man against man. Parliament against King. Catholic against Protestant . . . And out of the ruins . . . there'll be new things to believe in. New wars to be fought. And so it'll go on. Year after year. Like a rat devouring its own tail. With no possibility of any respite in the years to come. Not as far as I can see.

Struggling for control.

You can say what you like about tears . . . John . . . but they're not going to *change* the situation any. Are they? No amount of grief is going to make the slightest bit of difference. Come on. Be honest. Not when people's minds are made up. And their hearts are hardened.

A harsh shout of command. The sound is now much nearer.

Why can't we just forget our differences? That's what I'd like to know. Forget all the old hatreds. Prejudices. The scores we're supposed to settle . . . And start all over again. Like the dawn of a new day.

There is a sudden violent disturbance in the undergrowth and GEORGE *pushes his way through. A crown of leaves on his head. A livid gash on his leg. Hunched forward like an animal. Close behind him is a* GUARD, *holding him on a rope, which has been tied round his waist, binding his arms.*

JOHN. What's happening?

The GUARD *pushes him roughly forward with the blunt end of his halberd.* GEORGE *snarls back at him in pain and anger.*

But I can't see. I can't see!

KATHERINE. It's all right. It's all right. Nothing's going to happen. He's got him safe.

JOHN. Who's *who* got safe?

KATHERINE. The guard.

JOHN. What guard?

KATHERINE. Mr Cromwell's guard. He's got a prisoner with him.

JOHN. A prisoner?

KATHERINE. Yes. But he's tied up. He's harmless.

JOHN. Where? Where?

KATHERINE. Over there.

She turns him in the appropriate direction.

It's that half-naked old man. Remember? The carver who went mad.

GEORGE *jerks free of the rope, pulls the knife from his ragged waistband and circles around* OLIVER, *wildly gesticulating.*

GEORGE. You're a bloody carbuncle on the anus of the human condition! That's what you are, Cromwell. Do you hear? You should've been strangled at birth!

JOHN *seizes hold of* KATHERINE, *pulling her close.*

JOHN. I'm sorry, my love. I don't mean to panic.

KATHERINE. I know. I know.

GEORGE. You're nowt more'n a bandy-legged ape. Hanging on a witch's dug.

JOHN. But the darkness can seem terribly threatening.

GEORGE. A champion of Hell, crawling in the blood of your victims like a dog in a slaughterhouse.

He runs out of breath.

A fart blowing out of the bellows of your father's arse!

He sags forward. Resting his hands on his knees. The GUARD *strikes him in the back with the butt end of his halberd.* GEORGE *falls to the ground.*

Anyway. It's good to get it all off my chest. Mr Cromwell . . . I'm sure you'll understand.

The GUARD *hits him again.* KATHERINE *screams. He seems inert. But then he slowly turns and grins savagely at the* GUARD.

Is that the best you can do?

The GUARD *raises the halberd to strike him again.*

OLIVER. That's enough.

The GUARD *lowers the halberd.* OLIVER *advances on* GEORGE. *Standing just in front of him.*

Give me the knife. Handle towards me. That's right. Now push it along the ground.

GEORGE *does as he is told.*

KATHERINE. Why did you have to hit him so hard? A blow like that . . . It's a wonder you didn't break his back.

The GUARD *shrugs.*

GEORGE. Don't worry about me. I'll mend. Take more'n a shite like him to lay me low.

OLIVER. Take a good look, John. See how far a man can fall.

He picks up the knife.

For though most of us fall by the wayside in pursuit of grace, few will descend to the depths now reached by this piteous creature.

GEORGE. You're gloating, Cromwell. I'm disappointed. I thought you'd be above all that.

OLIVER. Caught trespassing, was he?

The GUARD *nods.*

And you're taking him into custody.

The GUARD *nods.*

How did he get the gash on his leg?

GEORGE. I got snagged up in one of your damn traps, Mr Cromwell. Yeah. This monstrously horrible contraption of springs and iron teeth. And I'll tell you something . . . if it hadn't been for a bit of old tree getting in the way, it would've sheared my leg clean off at the knee. Cruel things, them traps. Ought to be a law against them.

KATHERINE *edges forward towards him.*

KATHERINE. Is there anything I can do?

GEORGE. Thanks for your concern, young lady.

He examines his leg.

But I escaped lightly, all things considered. Lost a little blood is all.

He straightens up. Gingerly feeling his back.

KATHERINE. Are you thirsty? Would you like some water?

GEORGE. I am a bit dry. Yeah.

She digs the cup out of the hamper.

Nice to know that one of you at least . . . has a little
humanity.

KATHERINE *hurries to the stream and fills the cup with
water.*

JOHN. Where are you going?

KATHERINE. I'm just getting him some water. I won't be a
minute.

JOHN. I could do that.

But she's gone.

OLIVER. So you're finally caught, are you?

Silence.

GEORGE. That would seem to be the case. Yeah.

OLIVER. Well, it's not before time, I have to say. And I must
confess to a modest sense of relief in knowing that from
today I am no longer to be plagued by your most . . .
irritatious behaviour. Not that I'm rejoicing unduly. There
are plenty more where you came from. Malcontents and
troublemakers round every street corner.

KATHERINE *returns with a cup full of water.*

(*To* JOHN.) It's like sowing the Hydra's teeth. Cut down
one and another ten spring up in their place.

KATHERINE. Here you are.

She hands him the cup.

OLIVER. Don't get too close . . . whatever you do. Your
tender feelings . . . though in themselves laudable . . . are
perhaps a little misplaced.

GEORGE. Thanks, missus.

He drinks thirstily.

KATHERINE. There's more if you want it.

GEORGE. I'm quite restored. Thank you.

OLIVER. Where d'you get the knife from?

GEORGE. The knife?

He wipes his mouth dry.

It's hers. I took it from the hamper. Seemed like it might make a rather handy acquisition.

OLIVER. I thought as much.

He holds out the knife.

Here, Katherine. It's yours by rights. Why don't you put it back where it belongs?

KATHERINE. Thank you.

She takes the knife and returns it to the hamper.

GEORGE. It ain't just a weapon, you know . . . a knife. They have other uses . . . knives do.

He works his arms loose and rummages in the folds of his ragged waistband, pulling out a small carving.

See.

He holds it out awkwardly. Offering it to KATHERINE.

I made this for you.

KATHERINE *looks to* OLIVER. *Asking permission with her eyes to go and take the gift.*

OLIVER. Be careful.

GEORGE. I ain't going to try and take advantage, love. Ain't going to harm you. Here. Take it. Go on.

KATHERINE. For me?

He nods. KATHERINE *takes the carving.*

GEORGE. Yeah. I did it this afternoon. While listening to your aimless chatter. (*In a low voice.*) Between you and me, missus, you was the only one making any sense.

KATHERINE. It's beautiful. A head. A human head . . . with leaves coming out of his mouth.

GEORGE. It's what they call a 'green man'. Don't ask me why. There's one just like it in the church back home. About the only bit of carving to survive, as it happens.

KATHERINE. Survive?

GEORGE. Yeah. The day the soldiers came. With their axes.

KATHERINE. Oh yes . . .

GEORGE. And hacked out Heaven's likeness from the body of the church.

KATHERINE. Yes. I was told about that.

GEORGE. I watched it all, you know. From high in a tree. A vision of Hell. Men with the heads of birds. The heads of rats . . . tearing out the innards of the sanctuary below.

KATHERINE. How awful.

GEORGE. And after they'd gone . . . I just stood there. Among the wreckage. Rain streaming down my face. Nothing left of a lifetime's work . . . but blackened wood and smouldering ashes. Listening to the hiss and spit of the rain in the embers. And the echo of their psalms.

Silence.

OLIVER. Take him away.

The GUARD *roughly pushes* GEORGE *in the back. He totters forward a few paces and then stands firm.*

GEORGE. I've heard it said . . . Cromwell . . . you'd listen to any man . . . So long as he was speaking from the heart.

OLIVER. True enough. Yes.

GEORGE. Well then . . . listen. And listen good. I deserve it. All I been through. I think you'd have to agree.

OLIVER *remains impassive.*

I heard you talking just now. Trotting out all these big ideas. Talking as if you owned them. Just like you own property. Well, you don't own 'em. Ideas is for everyone. You can't pretend otherwise. Not after all we been through. You can't go back now. Chop down the Tree of Knowledge. It's too late. The word's got out! The leaves of the Bible's pages are open to us all!

JOHN. I don't think that's entirely –

GEORGE. Ideas have to grow. Don't you see? *Grow!* Like a tree grows. From the first seed. Spreading from the roots up to the leaves. And ideas you see . . . is only going to grow if they're shared by everyone. Everyone. Every living thing and fellow creature. Because we all belong. Don't you get it? All of us! Just as the leaves belong to the branch. As the branch belongs to the stem. And the stem to the roots.

The GUARD *starts pushing* GEORGE *out.* OLIVER *holds up a hand. He stops.*

God is the stem, of course, from which our nourishment mainly comes. You know . . . up from the ground. It's what gives us our strength. And if the world we live in is the branches . . . then art is the leaves. And by art I mean the making of beautiful things. Mainly with our hands. Our whole purpose in being, some would say. Our crowning glory.

Silence.

Hack off the leaves, Cromwell, and the whole tree dies. As you well know.

OLIVER. You've got trees growing in your brain.

GEORGE. True. I have. 'Swallowed an apple pip,' isn't that what they say?

He smiles.

Trees is what I know about, see. I carve their wood. I know their properties. Eat their fruits. Shelter under them. Live in them sometimes. Share my life with them. I mean, let's face it, to all intents and purposes . . . and I know this is going to sound a little strange . . . I am a bloody tree.

He stands with his arms outstretched like Leonardo's 'Universal Man'.

OLIVER. He's mad. Take him away.

He approaches OLIVER, *who looks him in the eyes and doesn't flinch.*

GEORGE. Here, Cromwell. You'd better have this.

The GUARD *lifts his halberd, ready to strike* GEORGE *in the back. But* OLIVER *motions him not to.*

You're king in all but name.

He takes off his crown of leaves and solemnly places it on OLIVER's *head.*

Nothing's changed, you know. Despite all the ructions of the Civil War. And all that happened after. It's the same people basically got their heels on our necks. Then as now. You just got different names and titles, that's all. Slid unnoticed into dead men's shoes.

OLIVER. Take him away!

The GUARD *pushes* GEORGE *out.* OLIVER *takes off the crown of leaves and sits down heavily.*

The trouble with these subversives . . . they think their ideas are going to change the world. What they don't realise is that it's the same mad drivel preached by every twopenny-ha'penny cheapjack up and down the country.

GEORGE *can be heard singing wildly in the distance.*

GEORGE (*off*).
When Adam delved and Eve span,
Who was then the gentleman?

OLIVER. How do we know they're not deep down . . . as greedy as everyone else? And all this egalitarian claptrap isn't just an illusion, a pretext, a facade, a cover . . . for much greedier ambitions, which they keep hidden even from themselves? And what they're really after is power. Pure and simple. So that once they've insinuated themselves into a position of authority, they can then quietly assume all the privileges and the property . . . above all, the *property* . . . of the people they're intending to replace. Who's to say . . . like ants infesting the very fabric of a house, sooner or later they won't bring the whole edifice crashing down about our ears?

A more distant echo of the song.

KATHERINE. Where's he taking him? What's going to happen?

OLIVER. He'll spend the night in the guardhouse. And then . . . in due course . . . Master Topcliffe will put him to the question. And if he's found to be mad . . . he'll spend the rest of his days in Bedlam, I shouldn't wonder. But if there's any sanity in the man at all . . . he'll be packed off to America . . . with the other grousers and malcontents.

He trudges over to JOHN, *who's sitting with his head in his hands, nudging him with his foot.*

What's the matter with you?

JOHN. Depressing, really.

OLIVER. What is?

No response.

Come on. Out with it. This isn't like you at all.

JOHN. He's got a point, don't you think? I mean, if there's no place for art . . . for craftsmanship . . . in this land of ours . . . then we're no better than savages. And our dreams are worthless. And our future . . . dust.

OLIVER. Oh. Cheer up, man. For pity's sake.

He tucks his shirt in his breeches. Ready for the off.

Let's get back to the house. Sit by the fireside. Share a pipe of tobacco, maybe. What do you say?

JOHN *sits resolutely where he is.*

I'm not against art, John. Don't get me wrong. And I'm not against dancing neither. As such. Or singing. Contrary to what many people believe. Or even drama, come to that. Of the right sort.

JOHN. I'm relieved to hear it.

OLIVER. But if you push me, I would have to say that what I am against . . . is the likeness, if you like . . . of a spiritual thing. And that's where I stick, I'm afraid. Come on, Kate. Pack your hamper and let's be off.

KATHERINE *fusses with the hamper.*

JOHN. But where does that leave me, for pity's sake?

OLIVER. What? What are you talking about? *What?*

JOHN. Me? What about me? For works of art are not all fashioned out of stone and wood. Paint and canvas. The likeness of God may just as well be fashioned in a poem as in a carving or an icon. Are you saying my work should be considered in the same way? And destroyed whenever it invokes the presence of Our Lord?

OLIVER. Don't be ridiculous.

JOHN. No. You see. Listen. It doesn't matter whether the presence of God is invoked in physical terms or in words . . . the impulse is the same.

OLIVER. I'm not going to argue. Let's go. Come on.

JOHN. What is a hymn if not an expression of worship and devotion? Could not a carving of Jesus be just the same? Fulfil the same function? Bring light to the darkest recess of the soul?

KATHERINE. John . . .

JOHN. You see, if you deny the power of poetic imagination, you deny the grandeur that lies dormant in us all. That part of ourselves that is prophetic. Our capacity for transcendence . . . our true potential . . . which I am convinced . . . can only finally find its true expression in the New Jerusalem . . . So tantalisingly near, it seems to me . . . when, like butterflies with crushed and dampened wings, slowly emerging from the chrysalis . . . we will finally evolve into the noble species we were ever destined to become.

OLIVER. Mmm.

Long silence.

Listening to you always makes me feel so grubby and prosaic. But then I remember that the reason you speak like this is because you're a poet. An artist. And artists . . . as a general rule, are a disreputable lot, whose personal morality – in my experience – never quite seems to match the dizzying heights of their dreams and aspirations. Which is some consolation, as you might well imagine, to us earth-bound souls.

He leans against a tree. Breathing deeply.

KATHERINE. You're not right, are you?

OLIVER. Right as I'll ever be, my dear. And mighty relieved to see the back of that madman . . . I don't mind telling you.

KATHERINE *picks up the hamper.*

KATHERINE. Will you be seeing your doctor these next few days?

OLIVER. I expect so. Yes. Why do you ask?

KATHERINE. Well . . . we were both thinking . . . John and I . . . that it might be a good idea if you got another opinion. That's right, isn't it, John?

No response.

OLIVER. I'm perfectly happy with Doctor Bate. I'd trust him with my life.

KATHERINE. All the same . . . It wouldn't do you any harm to talk to someone else. I mean, if there's anything in the remedies that isn't agreeing with you, he might know what it is.

OLIVER. You think it likely?

KATHERINE. It might be likely.

OLIVER. And if it's simply the natural consequence of an old man's failing constitution?

KATHERINE is distracted suddenly. Staring into the bushes.

Kate . . . I'm talking to you.

KATHERINE. Sorry. Well . . . Yes. I mean . . . that's likely too.

OLIVER. Thanks for your consideration. I'll think about it. I really will.

He stares at JOHN.

Are you coming, John?

No response.

Look. If you're not going to stir yourself, I'm going on ahead. I have things to do.

KATHERINE. We'll catch you up.

OLIVER *grunts a response. And trudges off.*

Silence.

JOHN. He's angry with me, isn't he?

KATHERINE. Mmm.

She stares once more into the bushes.

JOHN. You're very quiet.

KATHERINE. Yes.

JOHN. Is something the matter?

KATHERINE. I thought I saw someone.

JOHN. Thought you what?

KATHERINE. I was just vaguely staring into the trees over there . . . And I thought I saw someone. That's all. An old lady. Bending down to pick up a stick.

Silence. JOHN *puts on his jacket.*

But now I look again . . . I can see it's only my imagination. Branches in the wind.

He looks up. He hasn't been paying much attention to what she's been saying.

I'd like to go in now.

JOHN. Very well.

She picks up the hamper again.

Nature is a wild ungovernable thing. It's only by giving it a form . . . as the Athenians did . . . the Romans, too, in a less satisfactory way . . . that we begin to come to terms with it.

KATHERINE. I don't quite understand that.

JOHN. Without form . . . that is to say . . . without the
construct of our human brain impinging itself on the chaos
around us . . . there would be no culture. No art. No music.
Nothing.

KATHERINE. Mmm.

*She goes to him. Slips her hand through his arm. Kisses him
on the cheek. And together they walk arm in arm a little
way.*

He did listen to you, didn't he?

JOHN. Well, he certainly realised that I wasn't idly passing
the time of day.

They walk a little further.

But what decision the man will make . . . when the time
comes, I don't think even he knows.

KATHERINE. You didn't feel you were wasting your time?

JOHN. No. No. Far from it.

KATHERINE. It was a good day, wasn't it? A memorable day.

JOHN. Yes.

KATHERINE. One of those days we'll look back on in the
winter . . . huddled up in the January cold . . . and think,
'Was it really so hot we could sit out under the trees? And
eat our luncheon in the open air?'

JOHN. Yes. I know what you mean.

He laughs.

Actually, I don't believe one's effort is ever wasted.
Provided, of course, that God is still dwelling in one's heart.

He stops walking. And seems to be looking up into the sky.

I don't know how to put this. I feel I'm reaching for something that's just beyond my understanding. An idea I'm
sure future generations will come to understand in its
entirety. But when Christ comes again. For the second time.

He'll come . . . not as a single person . . . but as a whole community. I mean his identity won't be constrained by individuality . . . won't be confined to any one person. Not this time. He'll inhabit hundreds of people. Thousands, probably.

He smiles.

Living all together. In harmony. Freedom. And equality.

KATHERINE. I don't know. It sounds very beautiful. But I don't know.

She stares back into the woods as though seeing someone. Then quickly turns away.

You know that old woman I was telling you about? The one I saw in the trees?

JOHN. Go on.

KATHERINE. Well, it's not the first time. I've seen her before. Or I think I have, rather. Once I thought she was following me in the street. And on another occasion . . . Just before we met actually, I saw her through a window. A long way off. And she gave me an encouraging smile.

JOHN. Mmm.

KATHERINE. But one night she came to me in a dream. And took my baby away.

Silence.

JOHN. But you don't have a –

KATHERINE. I know. I know I don't. But I will have one day. And one day soon, I hope.

She leans into him. Putting an arm around his neck.

Don't worry, my love. It was only a dream.

And they walk away into the woods.

The End.

Historical Note

John Milton married Katherine a few months later, only for her to die in childbirth the following year. Milton himself lived on in blindness for another fifteen years, marrying for a third time.

Oliver Cromwell died two years later, in 1658. It was given out that he died of a 'tertian ague'. But in 1671, when Doctor Bate was himself on his deathbed, he confessed to giving Cromwell poison – a confession disregarded by most historians, as the delusory ravings of a man dying of syphilis.

A Nick Hern Book

Through a Cloud first published in Great Britain as a paperback original in 2004 by Nick Hern Books, 14 Larden Road, London W3 7ST, in association with the Drum Theatre Plymouth and Birmingham Rep

Through a Cloud copyright © 2004 Jack Shepherd

Jack Shepherd has asserted his right to be identified as the author of this work

Cover image: contemporary woodcut of the 1649 beheading of Charles I.

Typeset by Country Setting, Kingsdown, Kent CT14 8ES
Printed and bound in Great Britain by Cox and Wyman, Reading, Berks

A CIP catalogue record for this book is available from the British Library

ISBN 1 85459 844 9